Perspectives
on the Collections

OF **The New-York
Historical Society**

Perspectives
on the Collections

OF The New-York Historical Society

Introduction by Kenneth T. Jackson

THE HENRY LUCE III CENTER
for the Study of American Culture

THE NEW-YORK HISTORICAL SOCIETY 2000

Copyright ©2000 The New-York Historical Society

First Edition

All rights reserved. No part of this book may be used or reproduced in any manner
without written permission from the publisher.

This book, published in conjunction with the opening of the Henry Luce III Center
for the Study of American Culture, was made possible by the generous support of the
Henry Luce Foundation.

Library of Congress No. 00-107403

ISBN: 0-916141-05-5

The Henry Luce III Center for the Study of American Culture
The New-York Historical Society
Two West 77th Street
New York, NY 10024
www.nyhistory.org

MANAGING EDITOR: Nancy Eklund Later
BOOK DESIGN: Christine Stuermer and Melanie Roher of Roher/Sprague Partners
COVER PHOTOGRAPHY: Alan Orling

Printed in Canada

Table of Contents

ii   PREFACE

1   **New York and its Historical Society:**
      Two Centuries of Growth and Change

11   **Paintings, Miniatures, and Works on Paper**

53   **Sculpture**

69   **Furniture**

83   **Decorative Objects**

103   **Tools for Home and Trade**

113   **Private Life and Public Service**

141   FOR FURTHER READING

143   LIST OF FIGURES

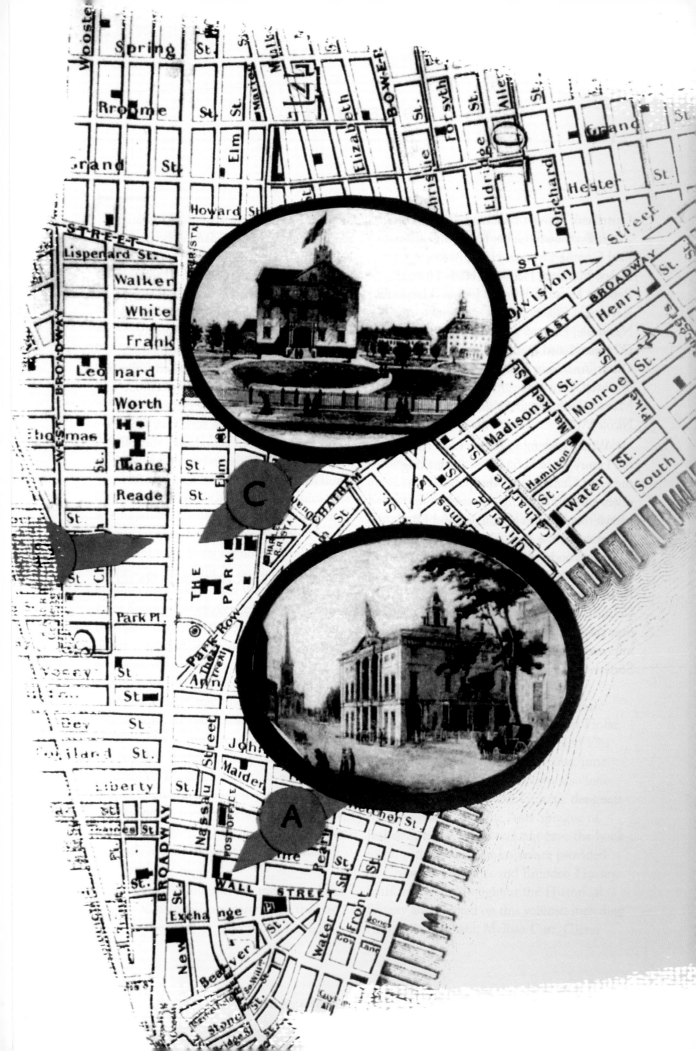

New York and Its Historical Society: Two Centuries of Growth and Change

On the early winter evening of November 20, 1804, a merchant named John Pintard gathered ten friends at the old City Hall, at the corner of Wall and Nassau streets, and founded the New-York Historical Society. This small group included Mayor DeWitt Clinton, Columbia professor David Hosack, Judge Egbert Benson, and merchant Anthony Bleecker, as well as three prominent ministers. Their purpose was nothing less than to "collect and preserve whatever may relate to the natural, civil, or ecclesiastical history of the United States in general and of this State in particular."

At the time the New-York Historical Society was created, the Barbary pirates were still wreaking havoc upon American shipping in the Mediterranean Sea, slavery was still legal in the Empire State, Noah Webster had not yet produced a dictionary, and Francis Scott Key had not yet written "The Star Spangled Banner." Michigan, Illinois, Missouri, Louisiana, Kansas, Iowa, Minnesota, and Texas were not yet states, and none of the great figures of the Civil War—Abraham Lincoln, Jefferson Davis, Ulysses S. Grant, Robert E. Lee, Thomas J. "Stonewall" Jackson, or William Tecumseh Sherman—had even been born. Meriwether Lewis and William Clark had embarked on their now-famous expedition to find an overland route to the Pacific Ocean, but at the very moment the Historical Society came into being, they had settled in for the winter just north of what is today Bismarck, North Dakota.

New York City was itself rather unimpressive in 1804. Its polyglot population of about 70,000 was clustered in modest houses south of Chambers Street. Manhattan's famous gridiron street system had not yet been visualized, let alone laid out. The total area of the municipality was less than a single square mile, and any able-bodied person could walk from one side of town to the other in a matter of minutes. At night, only the occasional clop-clop of horse's hooves or the footsteps of a solitary lamplighter broke the stillness. There was as yet no such thing as regular garbage pickup (wild pigs and dogs scavenged for food along the narrow roads) nor was there an adequate water supply system, paid professional firefighting, or an organized police force as we know it today. Greenwich Village was considered an outlying suburb, and places like Yorkville, Bloomingdale, and Harlem—all in Manhattan—were so far north as to represent completely separate settlements.

But by 1804, New York was already on its way to national dominance as an urban center. As early as 1789, it outdistanced its American rivals to become the leading city in domestic shipping. It exceeded Philadelphia in total tonnage in 1794, in the value of imports in 1796, and in exports in 1797. By 1820, Gotham had surpassed Mexico City as the largest metropolis in North America.

The backbone of Gotham's economy remained at the water's edge throughout the nineteenth century. The Port of New York ranked as the world's busiest from 1840 until 1950, when it was overtaken by Rotterdam. The value of its trade regularly exceeded that of Boston, Philadelphia, and Baltimore combined. Between 1830 and 1906, the harbor handled as much as 71 percent by value of the nation's annual foreign trade, a proportion more than triple that of its nearest competitor. Tramp steamers, sailing vessels, barges, and ferries populated its protected waterways, which were ideal for ocean-going vessels as well as smaller boats. Docks and piers loomed mile after mile up the Hudson and East rivers, along the shallow New Jersey and Staten Island shores, and from Greenpoint to Red Hook in Brooklyn. Beyond the docks stretched acres of warehouses, storage tanks, coal dumps, stone yards, sugar mills, breweries, dry docks, and ship chandlers. The city grew in size and waxed rich on the strength of its port, and became an *entrepôt* of power and culture within the New World.

A sophisticated economy emerged, with hundreds of thousands of longshoremen, laborers, and skilled craftsmen providing its underpinnings and multitudes of professionals steering its development. As national corporations took shape, New York became the headquarters for American business; by 1895, the city contained 298 mercantile and manufacturing firms worth more than one million dollars—more than Chicago, Boston, Philadelphia, San Francisco, Baltimore, and St. Louis combined. By 1900, Manhattan contained the largest concentrations of architects, bankers, lawyers, consulting engineers, industrial designers, and corporate officials on the continent. The Wall Street law firm had become a national institution, and investment bankers like J. P. Morgan, the Seligman brothers, and August Belmont were legendary.

Nowhere in the world were the symbols of wealth and power so abundant. According to an 1892 survey, New York and its suburbs contained almost two thousand millionaires, or 45 percent of the extreme-wealth holders in the United States. The "robber barons" of American industry—including John D. Rockefeller, Andrew Carnegie, and Frank W. Woolworth, who founded their empires elsewhere—moved to the giant city, as if to ratify their national significance. Manhattan became a kind of upscale Main Street to the nation and the streets of New York themselves became emblematic of the businesses they fostered—Wall Street for investment banking, Madison Avenue for advertising, Seventh Avenue for fashion, Fifth Avenue for elegant shops, and Broadway for entertainment.

New York had also achieved cultural dominance by the early twentieth century. A hub of communications, Gotham swept past Boston as the center of book and magazine publishing, and when radio was born in the 1920s, New York became home to the major networks. Broadway secured its place as the center of American theater, while the Metropolitan Museum of Art (founded in 1870), the Metropolitan Opera (1883), and the New York City Ballet (1948) set standards of artistic excellence matched only in Europe. Artists congregated in Greenwich Village. America's foremost writers made their homes throughout the city. Even in sports, New York dominated; Yankees Babe Ruth and Lou Gehrig led the nation's most famous sports franchise, and Madison Square Garden became the nation's foremost indoor sports arena.

In 1898, the municipality expanded beyond Manhattan to include Queens, Brooklyn, Staten Island, and the southern section of Westchester County, later known as the Bronx. In this five-borough form, Gotham continued to grow enormously, and by 1940—with a metropolitan population of more than eleven million—New York had become the largest and richest city in the world.

The founding of the New-York Historical Society was part of the larger effort to make New York the cultural as well as economic capital of the nation. When the Historical Society was created in 1804, several attempts to foster learned organizations within the Empire City had already been made, through the founding of such institutions as the Society for Encouraging Useful Knowledge, the Calliopean Society, the Uranian Society, the Belles Lettres Club, the Horanian Society, the Philological Society, the Friendly Club, and the New York Society for Promoting Agriculture, Arts and Manufactures. Of all these cultural organizations, only the Historical Society is still in operation today.

At its founding, the society put forward three fundamental goals: first, that it should strive to reach the general public, rather than merely an educated elite; second, that its collecting purview should be encyclopedic, rather than focused exclusively on New York; and third, that it should collect materials in many formats, including books, manuscripts, newspapers, fine arts, and artifacts, all of which were thought to have value for society at large. The Historical Society also made an early commitment to preserving objects that reflected everyday life in America—a bit of prescient curatorship, since during recent decades, this material has become critically important to cultural historians.

As a result of its broad mandate, the Historical Society's holdings grew rapidly. The vast influx of books, paintings, and artifacts created space problems, which at times hampered the organization's ability to make its collections accessible to the general public. The institution was forced to move six times during its first half-century, spending fifteen years as a tenant in the city's old almshouse, another fifteen years at New York University, and five years at the Stuyvesant Institute. Finally, in 1857, the Historical Society was able to move its collections—which included portrait paintings and sculptures, coins, medals, archeological and ethnological specimens, and some twenty-five thousand books and manuscripts—into its own building, located at Eleventh Street and Second Avenue.

In the ensuing years, the Historical Society's holdings continued to grow as a result of several major gifts, bequests, and purchases. In 1858, the Historical Society received the entire contents of the New-York Gallery of the Fine Arts, which included the collection of Luman Reed, a grocer-turned-entrepreneur who was widely

considered one of the city's most important patrons of the arts. Another impressive collection of fine arts was added in 1863, when the institution purchased 433 original watercolors by John James Audubon from his widow. At the time of the Audubon purchase, the Historical Society was the most significant art gallery in New York, exhibiting contemporary American art and Old Master paintings, as well as the artistic treasures of many ancient cultures. Egyptian mummies, Assyrian reliefs, and Incan artifacts were displayed against a backdrop of European paintings hung two and three rows high in the Historical Society's sky-lit galleries on Second Avenue. At the same time, the society sponsored sold-out lectures by such luminaries as novelist Herman Melville, newspaperman Horace Greeley, statesman Daniel Webster, and historian George Bancroft, rendering the institution a center for intellectual as well as artistic activity in the city.

In the five decades that followed the Civil War, however, the Historical Society lost its edge as a local cultural leader and instead became something of a backward-looking institution in a forward-moving metropolis. This was due to a number of related circum-

MAP OF LOWER MANHATTAN *showing the locations and façades of the New-York Historical Society's successive homes between 1804 and 1908. Print Room, Pictorial Archives, #37725*

stances. The Historical Society's collections expanded beyond the capacity of its Second Avenue facility to house them. Unable to raise the funds necessary to build larger quarters, the society was forced to decline the offer made by New York State of free land in newly opened Central Park. Upstart competitors like the Metropolitan Museum of Art, which *did* take the state up on its offer, and the Metropolitan Opera pushed history—the primary product of the Historical Society—off center stage. At the same time, the society resisted the swelling movement to professionalize standards in library administration and historical research and acquiesced to functioning as a haven for amateur genealogists. Most significantly, the society shunned government funding and committed itself to pursuing only private support to cover its expenditures. This became problematic in the twentieth century, when other research institutions like the New York Public Library began receiving tax funds. By the time the Historical Society petitioned for state assistance at the end of the nineteenth century, it was almost too late.

Solutions to some of the society's problems were soon found. With the help of Henry Dexter (an author, philanthropist, and president of the American News Company), and Samuel Verplanck Hoffman (a real estate mogul who devoted almost forty years to the Historical Society as its president and chairman of the trustees), the institution purchased lots on Central Park West between 76th and 77th streets, then the northern edge of the growing city. In 1908, the Historical Society opened the magnificent beaux-arts structure in which it still resides today. The palazzo-like building provided both sufficient gallery space for art and artifacts in the museum collections and an elegant, sky-lit reading room for the library. Beginning in 1935, two wings were added to the building, expanding it north and south to encompass the entire length of the block.

The New-York Historical Society was on a roll. Between 1935 and 1942, a bequest of $4.5 million from the children of former New York Life Insurance Company president David Thompson enabled the society to address some of its more entrenched problems. This windfall—equal to over sixty million dollars in today's currency—allowed Alexander J. Wall, then head of the Historical Society, to expand the salaried staff from seven to seventy-five

View of the New-York Gallery of the Fine Arts, *installed in the Historical Society's Second Avenue building after 1867, featuring a marble statue of "Ruth" by Brooklyn sculptor Henry Kirke Brown. Print Room, Pictorial Archives, #198*

people, to move the organization back into the professional mainstream of librarians and historians, and to continue to offer the public free access to its treasures. The Historical Society's comprehensive library once again became a routine stop for scholars and doctoral students researching New York, as well as American, history. Under Wall's leadership, the hybrid character of the institution—with its inter-related museum and library collections—remained a distinguishing feature and source of great strength.

Despite the achievements made possible through the help of Dexter, Hoffman, and the Thompsons, after World War II the organization experienced continued financial and space problems. R. W. G. Vail, who led the Historical Society after 1960, was an outstanding scholar, but he was neither a skilled nor enthusiastic administrator. Moreover, the society continued to accept almost anything and everything offered to it, without concern for quality or regard to whether such acquisitions would contribute to the institution's overall mission. By the end of the 1960s, revenues failed to keep pace with expenditures, especially when stock-market investments began their downward spiral.

By the late 1980s, the Historical Society was regularly running a seven-digit deficit, forcing the trustees to erode the institution's relatively small endowment to cover expenses. Even with such liberal spending, the Historical Society proved unable to give proper care to its now-enormous collections, parts of which were stored at an off-site facility that did not meet professional conservation standards. In fact, a confidential trustees' report that fell into the hands of the *New York Times* revealed that a few of the society's valuable paintings had been allowed to deteriorate.

The Historical Society struggled to respond to these desperate circumstances. The organization had already ceased publication of the *New-York Historical Society Quarterly* in 1979 as a cost-cutting measure, ending a proud run of more than six decades. In 1988, it laid off one-quarter of its employees and announced plans to sell about forty European paintings no longer considered to be within the scope of its mission. The professional museum community reacted angrily to this plan to deaccession works of art, especially in light of the fact that the Attorney General of New York State granted "one-time" permission to the Historical Society to reinvest proceeds from those sales into its general operating budget. This ran counter to accepted museum guidelines that insisted such proceeds be used to care for existing collections or for the acquisition of additional works of art. Curators worried that this special dispensation would set a dangerous precedent and encourage other cash-strapped museums to claim that they, too, needed to sell off their patrimony to pay the light bills. At the same time, the Attorney General's Office launched an investigation into "whether the art collection [was] being properly cared for and what legal consequences that may have."

Under the determined leadership of Barbara Knowles Debs, the former president of Manhattanville College who became the director of the Historical Society in 1988, the institution seemed about to turn the corner on renewed prosperity. But an avalanche of public criticism, combined with the reduction in the endowment, had so weakened the organization that on January 1, 1993, the trustees reluctantly suspended public access to its museum collections. The other shoe dropped on February 4, 1993, when the *New York Times* reported simply:

> The board of the New-York Historical Society voted yesterday to shut down the institution's library on February 19. All public programs are to be canceled, with the exception of a traveling show of 90 Audubon watercolors that had long been planned, and 41 staff members will be dismissed; a skeleton crew of 35 will be left to handle security, conservation and disposition of the collections.

The situation was clearly desperate: collections of books, paintings, manuscripts, and artifacts that had been painstakingly acquired over almost two centuries were at risk of being dispersed, no longer to be safeguarded as a resource for scholars or the general public. Out of money and no longer able to fulfill its mission, the New-York Historical Society was in danger of dissolution.

Fortunately, help came from many directions. Governor Mario Cuomo praised the Historical

Society as "a vital part of the cultural heritage of New York State." The *New York Times* editorialized that the collections were an irreplaceable part of the city's cultural memory, and six hundred scholars from around the nation signed a petition asking for the municipal and state governments to find a way to "keep the collections intact and available to New Yorkers." More importantly, in 1994 a new leadership team, led by President Betsy Gotbaum and Chairman of the Board of Trustees Miner Warner, was set in place. Together, they refined the institution's mission statement, limiting its collecting efforts to New York-related materials. They also re-invigorated the board, reorganized the staff, and initiated a major fund-raising campaign, which successfully brought in millions of dollars from New York City and State to pay for much-needed capital improvements such as repairs to the Society's leaking roof. A one-time agreement with the Attorney General that permitted the sale of deaccessioned duplicates and items that no longer related to the Historical Society's revised mission generated additional funds for the crippled endowment. In a culminating show of faith, the Henry Luce Foundation contributed $7.5 million to enable the society to develop a new facility that would make available, in a single place and to a larger audience, items from its vast museum collections. Seven years after New York's oldest cultural institution had been teetering on the edge of collapse, the Historical Society emerged stronger than ever and better equipped to serve as the guardian of the cultural memory of the city and state.

With the creation of the Henry Luce III Center for the Study of American Culture, the strengths of the New-York Historical Society's museum collection are being rediscovered. Occupying the entire fourth floor of the Historical Society's landmark building on Central Park West, the Luce Center houses and displays nearly forty thousand objects, organized in categories that range from paintings, sculpture, furniture, and silver, to archeological fragments, military arms, fire-fighting equipment, and farm implements. The size and diversity of the organization's holdings are readily apparent as one walks among the display cases and views the collections up close. Incomparable works of art and everyday objects,

spanning the colonial period to the present, are housed side by side, at times resulting in some startling juxtapositions: a rare piece of early New York silver is exhibited at close proximity to the original model of the Civil War ironclad *Monitor*, not far from the world's foremost collection of Tiffany lamps. Reunited under a single roof in a state-of-the-art, climate-controlled environment, the museum collections are safely housed in compliance with the latest conservation standards as a result of the Luce Foundation's magnificent gift.

No longer a simple repository, the Historical Society's museum has been transformed into a laboratory for generating ideas. The Luce Center elevates the study of art and artifacts to a central place within historical research. In the past, historians have relied on paper records for most of their evidence regarding the life and times of earlier generations; only in recent decades have they developed an appreciation for physical objects—the material culture of a people— and how they might be used to generate new historical insights. Many scholars now consider artifacts to be important evidence of how people conducted their public and private lives, of their evolving ideas about home and family life, of the development of technology, and of the growth of local and national sentiment. Others see them as records of changes in taste or style, of craftsmanship, or of the history of collecting. The stories behind the artifacts housed in the Luce Center are as varied as the artifacts themselves: each provides a window on New York's past.

The Luce Center's open plan allows for free and unscripted movement to encourage browsing, independent research, and exploration. But for those less familiar with the kinds of stories objects tell, a series of interpretive tools designed for guided and focused inquiry are also available. Hand-held guides provide perspectives on collections categories and help visitors understand objects on display. Special exhibits placed throughout the center suggest themes that relate to objects in the collection such as "Leaving a Legacy," the way that objects become infused with meaning as they pass from one generation to the next. Audio tours create narrative pathways through the center, linking objects across diverse

READING ROOM *of the Historical Society's library at 170 Central Park West, around 1950. Print Room, Pictorial Archives, #7284*

media in order to highlight topics like "New York History," or "Puzzles & Mysteries." These structured experiences are designed to illustrate the variety of ways art and artifacts in the Luce Center can be used to reflect upon the history of a people, a city, and even a nation.

Also available are tools designed to help visitors access the combined resources of the Historical Society's museum and library collections. User-friendly computer terminals positioned throughout the Luce Center provide a catalogue of museum objects. Eventually cross-referenced to the library's holdings, this catalogue will bring to bear one of the nation's richest storehouses of American historical material on our understanding of the museum collections. Two million manuscripts and 350,000 books are currently held by the library, along with countless maps, atlases, photographs, engravings, broadsides, sheet music, and the drawings and archives of famous American

architects Alexander Jackson Davis, Cass Gilbert, and Stanford White. These materials provide key contexts for the interpretation of museum objects and, with the creation of the Luce Center and its computerized catalogue, are now held in unprecedented proximity to that collection.

Like those tools, this book itself constitutes a guide to interpreting the art and artifacts in the Luce Center. Using information drawn largely from the Historical Society's resources, it reveals the histories of seventy-five objects in the museum collections and is designed to encourage visitors to engage them on a variety of levels.

Often the most compelling thing about a work of art or artifact is not its physical appearance or style, but instead what can be inferred about the social, political, and economic forces that helped shape it and that it, in turn, helped shape. A few examples from the Luce Center's collections come to mind:

Furniture, on view in the Henry Luce III Center for the Study of American Culture.
Photograph courtesy Alan Orling.

THE LIKENESSES OF important individuals housed in the museum's extensive collection of portraits, miniatures, sculptures, and death masks lead to reflection on the relationship of these individuals to the life and history of New York City and the nation. Death masks of George Washington, whose first year as President was spent in New York City, Abraham Lincoln, who gave a career-making speech at Cooper Union, and General William Tecumseh Sherman, who failed as a banker in the city before going on to Civil War notoriety, remind us of the many ways in which the nation's most powerful citizens have participated in the life of New York City.

NUMEROUS PAINTINGS and decorative arts can be used to interpret a particular time in New York's history. The painting of the Tontine Coffee House illustrates one of the city's busiest commercial corners at the turn of the nineteenth century. It brings to mind the fact that importation and processing of coffee was an important factor in Gotham's domination of the nation's maritime trade during the nineteenth century. It also documents an interesting social pattern in the young port city, where fast-breaking news was reported and discussed in coffee houses; in doing so, the painting records the importance of dining out and enjoying the company of others in a public setting, which was originally related to the creation of wealth in burgeoning cities.

THE LUCE CENTER'S copious collection of tables and chairs, chests and sofas, remind us that Gotham was once renowned for its talented craftsmen, many of whom—like Duncan Phyfe and Charles-Honoré Lannuier—produced objects of lasting value. Although most people think of Chicago, Pittsburgh, and Southern California as the traditional centers of American industry, New York was in fact the world's leading manufacturing city until 1950. The city achieved such prominence, not because of an abundance of huge blast furnaces or long assembly lines, but because of its concentration of many thousands of small enterprises, like furniture makers and textile manufacturers. These outfits generally employed fewer than a dozen persons and required relatively little space, yet together they employed more industrial workers and accounted for more value added by manufacture than any other municipality.

BY STUDYING *The Intelligence Office*, William Henry Burr's 1849 painting of an employment agency, one can analyze the social hierarchy and class divisions inherent in nineteenth-century American society. The painting, which features immigrant women recently arrived, perhaps from Ireland, documents the importance of New York City as a port of entry for millions of immigrants, who arrived on teeming ships from the mid-nineteenth century until World War II. The painting also reminds us that New York City has always been a place of extreme economic divisions and that the abolition of slavery in the city did not mean the end of human exploitation. The vision of young women being auctioned off in a version of wage slavery is evocative of both the promise of the metropolis, which offered those who wanted to work at least the hope of a better life, and its darker side—for many, the climb up the ladder was lonely and unrewarding.

A HUMBLE WOODEN BARREL, on view in the Luce Center, signals one of the most important events in the history of the city. The 1825 opening of the Erie Canal, the final link in an all-water route that flowed from the country's interior down the Hudson River to the Atlantic Ocean, insured New York's pre-eminence as a port of national and international trade. At the ceremony celebrating the opening of the canal, Governor DeWitt Clinton used this barrel to pour water from the Great Lakes into the Atlantic off the shores of Sandy Hook, symbolically uniting the markets of the Midwest with those of the growing metropolis and linking them, through previously established trade routes, to those across the ocean.

Visitors to the Luce Center will formulate their own list of favorite objects and will draw their own connections between those objects and the rich history of New York City and State, connections that may lead to entirely new insights. In elevating art and artifacts to a prominent position in the field of historical research, the Luce Center commemorates the wisdom of the founders of the New-York Historical Society, who shared a faith that even in a rapidly developing city that embraced progress and readily sacrificed the past to the future, history could inform modern civilization and instruct future generations. As the Historical Society looks forward to its third century of service, the Luce Center returns the institution to the mainstays of its original mission—that the general public and scholars alike be encouraged to draw important insights about New York's history from their encounters with art and artifacts from its past.

Portrait from 1796 of the Seneca Chief Ki-On-Twog-Ky *wearing gifts presented to him by the "Council of the Thirteen Fires" in New York. Gift of Thomas Jefferson Bryan, 1867.314*

Making Peace with Ki-On-Twog-Ky

A RANKING CHIEF of the Seneca tribe, Gyantwachia, Ki-On-Twog-Ky (1732/40-1836), also known as Cornplanter, proudly wears a silver medal around his neck, a pair of silver armbands, and a scarlet stroud around his shoulders. This regalia was presented to the chief by the United States Congress during his May 1786 visit to New York, then the nation's capital. Congress presented these items, along with two pounds of vermillion, six dozen brooches, a laced coat and vest, two ruffled shirts, and other items of dress, as a token of its respect and good will. Chief Cornplanter is thought to have remained in the capital after his meeting to sit for this portrait, painted by the artist F. Bartoli (active 1783–about 1796).

Chief Cornplanter had sought out the "Council of the Thirteen Fires" over his concern about the establishment of British settlements at Niagara, just north of his lands. Were British and American hostilities to resume over Britain's failure to withdraw into Canada, the peace of his villages was sure to be disrupted. Along with these gifts, Congress gave Chief Cornplanter its assurance that both the British and the Americans wanted to live in peace with Native Americans and would respect the boundaries of land assigned to them by treaty.

Congress had good reason to placate their visitor with valuable gifts and promises of respectful relations. Chief Cornplanter had earned his reputation as a great warrior and influential chief of the confederated Iroquois tribes, which for centuries had occupied the territory between Lake Champlain and the Genesee River. During the American Revolution, these tribes—by then clustered on the New York-Pennsylvania border along the Allegheny River—sided with the British, electing Chief Cornplanter as their leader. Commissioned as a captain by the British, Chief Cornplanter led the western Senecas in raids against American outposts and settlements. He became a scourge of frontier settlers, especially in Pennsylvania's Wyoming Valley and in the Cherry and Mohawk valleys of New York. By 1796—the year of this painting—Chief Cornplanter had taken over the civil leadership of his people, and his presence in the area represented a continued threat to new settlers.

Some scholars suggest that the smoking pipe featured in Bartoli's painting signals the establishment of peaceful relations between Chief Cornplanter and the young republic. In his 1786 meeting with Congress, he was persuaded to throw in his lot with the Americans in exchange for the protection of his lands. President George Washington rewarded Cornplanter's friendship and good service in 1794, when he signed a treaty in Philadelphia further securing Indian claims, and thereby establishing a more lasting peace between the United States and the various Iroquois tribes.

Whatever the artist's symbolic intention with Chief Cornplanter's pipe, the nation's respect for its treaties with the Indian population ultimately would not hold. In 1958, the U.S. District Court took the Iroquois's land grant by right of eminent domain to make way for the construction of a dam to contain the waters of the Allegheny.

Coffee Culture, Then as Now

SOMETIME AROUND THE close of the eighteenth century, in the midst of the heavily trafficked intersection of Wall and Water streets, Francis Guy (1760-1820) pitched a tent and climbed in. The artist stretched a piece of black gauze over the tent's only window, picked up a piece of chalk, and carefully outlined the scene that appeared through the fabric. Guy later transferred these markings to canvas and painted one of the most compelling streetscapes of old Manhattan to have survived from the period.

Guy's view looks north along Water Street and east along Wall. On the left side of the canvas stands the Tontine Coffee House; on the right, diagonally across the intersection, stands the Merchants' Coffee House. The view down Wall Street extends to the East River to include sailing ships tied to the wharves, where longshoremen unloaded one hundred and sixty-pound bags of coffee beans, imported from South America. Over the next century, New York would emerge as the leading importer and processor of coffee beans in the world.

But just as important as the beverage served in these establishments was the public life they encouraged. Coffee houses acted as important meeting places in eighteenth-century America, just as they had in England and Amsterdam centuries earlier. Politicians and military officers congregated there to exchange ideas, and merchants gathered over coffee to transact vital business. The Tontine Coffee House, one of the best-known establishments of its kind in New York, functioned as a marketplace for all types of commodities, including ships, horses, real estate, and even slaves.

In fact, the Tontine Coffee House was constructed by stockbrokers looking for a place to trade. In the winter of 1792/3, a group of brokers at the Merchant's Coffee House decided to build a space of their own. Fearing they had too little business to warrant building a stock exchange, they built a coffee house instead. The name 'tontine' derives from the type of financial arrangement used to bankroll this enterprise: a cross between a life insurance policy and legalized gambling, a tontine was an agreement between a

Francis Guy's painting of THE TONTINE COFFEE HOUSE *documents the center of New York's commercial life around 1800. Purchased by the society, 1907.32*

group of investors to purchase stock and sell it at a later date, splitting the profits among a specified number of surviving investors. In the case of the Tontine Coffee House, shares were offered to investors at two hundred dollars apiece, and the coffee house was built with the proceeds. When, by the terms of the tontine, only seven lucky shareholders remained, the property was sold and the proceeds distributed among them.

The 'tontine' has long been outlawed and the brokers who once met at the Tontine Coffee House have settled into new quarters at the New York Stock Exchange. But, the intersection of Wall and Water streets still occupies the heart of New York's busy Financial District, and, like the figures in Guy's painting, New Yorkers still flock to coffee houses—and cyber-cafes—to drink coffee, conduct business, and trade ideas today.

Exiles and Immigrants

ANNE-MARGUÉRITE-HENRIETTE ROUILLÉ DE MARIGNY, Baroness Hyde de Neuville (about 1749-1849), made this sketch at the *École Économique*, or Economical School, in New York City between 1810 and 1814. Executed in black chalk and graphite on blue paper, the small, delicate drawing depicts a student working at his desk. The sketch is one in a group of nineteen that records adults and children reading and writing, carrying out chores, and doing handiwork. Drawn on loose sheets and executed at different scales with various degrees of finish, the sketches have the quality of a personal diary, recording in broad strokes and minute detail the character of daily life at the Economical School.

In 1806, the baroness and her husband— an ardent royalist dedicated to the restoration of the Bourbon monarchy—chose exile in the United States over loyalty to the Emperor Napoleon. Four years later, the Hydes de Neuville founded the Economical School with a group of upper-class French exiles, the Baron serving as its first secretary. The school was established to give aid and affordable instruction to the children of less fortunate immigrants from France and from French-speaking colonies such as Santo

A STUDENT *at New York's Economical School, sketched by Baroness Hyde de Neuville, between 1810 and 1814. Purchased by the Society, 1953.274f*

Domingo. Many of these families, like the Hydes de Neuville, had come to New York as political refugees, forced by civil unrest to leave their native countries. Some experienced great reversals of fortune and arrived in the city destitute, dependent on public and private charity. When the Economical School opened in 1810, it enrolled more than two hundred impoverished students. Hyde de Neuville's sketches from the school record, simply and candidly, the experience of this immigrant class, as viewed by another.

The grid that organizes the proportions of the finely drawn face of this student at the Economical School signals Hyde de Neuville's academic training. As a member of an aristocratic family, the baroness probably received private drawing lessons from a master while growing up in France. During her thirteen years in the United States, she used her considerable skills to execute hundreds of drawings and watercolors, eighty-eight of which are held in the New-York Historical Society's collection. In addition to life at the Economical School, her work documents the everyday experiences of family members and friends, sailors and chambermaids, and provides an early look at a new social order developing within the young republic.

Illustrating the "Animal 'Man'"

IN AN AGE before photography or television, a portrait of Thomas Jefferson (1743-1826) painted by Rembrandt Peale (1778-1860) in 1800 gave Americans one of their first glimpses of the man they would elect twice as president. Peale's portrait of Jefferson, circulated widely in the form of engravings and lithographs, became one of the country's best-remembered images of Jefferson. In 1805, Peale painted a second portrait of Jefferson, and although it is considered a true likeness—indeed, one of Peale's finest works—it has never achieved the same prominence in the nation's collective visual memory. But in representing Jefferson, the second portrait served a different purpose.

Rembrandt Peale painted the 1805 portrait of Thomas Jefferson to hang in the portrait gallery of his father's house in Philadelphia. After returning from the Revolutionary War, Charles Willson Peale (1741-1827), a distinguished painter in his own right, had opened a small public gallery in his home, where he exhibited mostly his own work. During the final years of the war, Peale began to record the faces of America's heroes, both in gratitude for their service and as *exempla virtutis* for the young nation.

Jefferson's reputation as a statesman had been firmly established long before the Peales chose to paint him. His role in the Revolution—as member of the Continental Congress and as author of the Declaration of Independence—easily qualified him for a spot in Peale's portrait gallery. By 1805, his political accomplishments also included stints as governor of Virginia, minister to France, secretary of state, vice-president, and President of the United States. But by the time Jefferson's 1805 portrait was completed, Peale's Portrait Gallery had been incorporated into the broader and more complex framework of the Peale Museum. Founded in 1786, the museum combined the interests of art with those of science: like a seventeenth-century cabinet of curiosities, it was filled not only with paintings but with mineralogical and ethnological material, as well as natural specimens collected from all over America and arranged according to genus and species. Jefferson's portrait joined the double row of uniform-size works illustrating "the Animal 'Man,'" which hung above stuffed birds of all varieties, skinned, cleaned, and mounted by the elder Peale and perched in front of realistically painted scenery. The placement of the portrait probably appealed to the President. The ultimate Renaissance man, Jefferson shared an avid interest in science with his friend Charles Willson Peale. A dedicated naturalist, scientist, geographer, surveyor, botanist, ethnologist, and paleontologist, Jefferson's interest in science would eventually prompt him to donate the ethnological and natural specimens collected by Lewis and Clark to the Peale Museum.

By 1810, the Peales expanded the definition of "the Animal 'Man'" to include scientists, chemists, botanists, and even other artists. What had begun as a portrait gallery commemorating the nation's statesmen and military heroes had become a museum representing "a world in miniature," honoring distinguished men from all disciplines as "but one part of God's great scheme of things."

Rembrandt Peale's 1805 portrait of THOMAS JEFFERSON, *painted to hang in the Peale Museum in Philadelphia. Gift of Thomas Jefferson Bryan, 1867.306*

Portrait of the Artist as Naturalist

AFTER TRAINING IN the London studio of the famous American expatriate painter Benjamin West, Charles Willson Peale (1741-1827) established himself as a portraitist in Philadelphia. When he turned his business over to his son Rembrandt in 1795, he was a nationally recognized artist. But at the end of his life, when asked to paint a self-portrait to hang in the Pennsylvania Academy of Fine Arts—an institution Peale helped to found in 1791 to cultivate the fine arts and to invigorate the talents of artists in the new republic—Peale chose to represent himself not as an artist, but as a man of science.

Peale's 1824 self-portrait shows him not with brush in hand, as had earlier self-portraits, but leaning against the large bone of a mastodon. In 1801, as a member of a national committee elected to collect scientific specimens throughout the country, Peale unearthed the skeletal remains of two fossilized mastodons from a glacial bog near Newburgh, New York. The bones of the enormous creatures were shipped to Philadelphia, where the mastodons were reconstructed, bone by bone. One was placed on exhibit in the "Mammoth Room" of the Peale Museum, an extraordinary place filled with art and natural specimens that had grown out of the painter's small portrait gallery; the other toured Europe with one of Peale's sons. Eleven feet tall, fifteen feet long, and sporting eleven-foot tusks, Peale's mastodons offered the world its first glimpse of the "great American *incognitum*," which had roamed the continent long before the arrival of man. Young Federalists, keenly aware of the republic's artistic and cultural infancy, celebrated Peale's find as evidence of the antiquity of America.

The mystery of the great mastodon had been introduced to Peale some twenty years earlier and had played an important role in the founding of the Peale Museum. In 1783, the artist had been commissioned to illustrate a large collection of bones from an as-yet-unidentified creature discovered on the Ohio River. Peale's brother-in-law Colonel Nathaniel Ramsay visited the artist's studio and, fascinated by the giant bones, claimed he would have gladly paid good money to see them. He added that he

Charles Willson Peale's SELF PORTRAIT WITH MASTODON BONE *of 1824. Purchased by the New-York Historical Society, 1940.202*

found them infinitely more interesting than the portraits of national heroes Peale exhibited in his gallery. Ramsay's not-so-tactful comments planted the seed for what became, in 1786, Peale's combination art and natural history museum. In his 1824 *Self Portrait with Mastodon Bone*, Peale ultimately pays tribute both to the founding of his museum and to his discovery of the ancient creature—his great contribution to natural science.

From Slave to Saint

PAINTINGS FROM THE early decades of the nineteenth century that feature African Americans usually depict scenes of slavery and plantation life; these portrait miniatures, however, deviate from that norm. Here, Pierre Toussaint (1766-1853), his wife Juliette Noel (about 1786-1851), and their adopted daughter Euphemia (1815-1829) are portrayed as affluent members of society. Their fashionable clothing and jewelry attest to the wealth and social position the family had attained in New York by the 1820s, when these miniatures were painted. In fact, the very existence of the portraits, created by the Italian painter Anthony Meucci (1808-1889), confirms the family's status: miniatures were one of the most treasured forms of jewelry in Federal America, custom-made as private mementos to be worn or carried by a loved one.

Judging only by these portraits, it would be hard to guess that Pierre Toussaint began his life as a slave. Toussaint was born on the Haitian plantation of wealthy landowner Jean Berard. When Berard and his wife fled political unrest on the island around 1787, they brought Toussaint and other slaves to New York City with them. Toussaint's masters treated him relatively well: he was apprenticed to Madame Berard's professional hairdresser and was even allowed to keep some of his earnings. In 1791, however, the Berards' fortunes changed. Mr. Berard returned to Haiti to discover his plantation had been destroyed and his once-considerable fortune, dissolved. He died suddenly on the island, leaving his wife and child impoverished.

In a remarkable act of kindness, Toussaint began secretly supporting Berard's family with his wages. Hairdressing had proven a lucrative profession for Toussaint; his clients were among New York's wealthiest ladies—many of whom spent as much as a thousand dollars a year on their coiffure. He assisted Madame Berard for over fifteen years—while continuing to serve as her slave—until 1807, when from her deathbed she freed Toussaint.

Toussaint could have purchased his own freedom years earlier. Instead, he used his income to buy freedom for dozens of other slaves, including his future wife and his sister, Rosalie. When Rosalie died of tuberculosis, Toussaint and his wife adopted her daughter, Euphemia, though she, too, died from the disease, at the age of fourteen. As a free man, Toussaint continued his charitable

From left to right: Portrait miniatures of PIERRE TOUSSAINT, EUPHEMIA TOUSSAINT *and* MRS. PIERRE TOUSSAINT, *all by Anthony Meucci, from about 1825. Gift of Miss Georgina Schuyler, 1920.4, 1920.6, and 1920.5, respectively*

works, taking in other orphaned children, aiding cholera victims, giving lavishly to many of the city's poor churches, and supporting its first black school.

When Toussaint died in 1853, his body was placed on top of his relatives within a single grave in the cemetery of Old St. Patrick's Church, in today's Little Italy. About a century later, his remains were exhumed by the Archdiocese of New York and re-interred beneath the high altar of St. Patrick's Cathedral, where they now keep company with those of other important figures, such as Cardinal John O'Connor (1920-2000). In light of his good works, the Roman Catholic Church has begun a campaign to canonize Toussaint.

One of only two known representations of Toussaint, this miniature portrait has become an important record of the man who might become the first black American saint of the Roman Catholic Church. But equally important, Toussaint's miniature—and those of his family—testify to its subject's extraordinary life and exceptional generosity of spirit.

Recording Nature, Preserving Art

HOPING TO "verify one of those astonishing fits of nature," John James Audubon (1785-1851) traveled to Louisiana in December of 1825 to paint the Carolina parakeet. His watercolor captures the brilliantly colored, engagingly antic birds feeding on the cocklebur. At the time, the Carolina parakeet inhabited the mature, deciduous forests from the Great Lakes south to Florida and from Colorado east to the Atlantic. "The richness of their plumage, their beautiful mode of flight, and even their screams," Audubon wrote in 1842, "afford welcome intimation that our darkest forests and most sequestered swamps are not destitute of charms."

> *"It is somewhat singular that my enthusiastic husband struggled to have his labours published in his Country and could not; and I have struggled to sell his forty years of labour and cannot."*
>
> —Mrs. John J. Audubon, 1862

But by the 1840s, westward expansion had begun to endanger Audubon's beloved parakeet, the only parrot native to the United States. Deprived of their natural habitat, the birds began to disappear. Hunters exacerbated the problem, decimating the flocks in droves, for food, feathers, or simply for sport. In 1920, the once-abundant Carolina parakeet was sighted in the wild for the last time. The species is now extinct.

No one will ever see the birds of America first-hand, the way Audubon encountered and recorded them. For four decades, he documented in watercolor, pastel, pencil, and ink, the looks and habits of many now-extinct or extremely rare birds, including the swallow-tailed kite, the whooping crane, the passenger pigeon, and the bald eagle. His drawings were recognized during his lifetime as both important documents of natural history and as amazing works of art. Today, Audubon is still revered as the most gifted naturalist-illustrators of the nineteenth century.

Given this appreciation for Audubon's work, it is hard to believe that, following the artist's death, his widow, Lucy, had trouble finding a repository for her husband's legacy. In 1862, Mrs. Audubon offered the New-York Historical Society the original drawings used to produce Audubon's seminal work, *The Birds of America*, published in London between 1827 and 1838. The asking price was beyond the Historical Society's resources and had to be raised through an appeal to individual donors. A year passed. Mrs. Audubon pleaded with the Historical Society's librarian to buy the drawings in order to prevent them from ending up at the British Museum, which had expressed an interest in acquiring them. But the Historical Society still could not afford the purchase. Dismayed, Mrs. Audubon wrote to the organization's president, "It is somewhat singular that my enthusiastic husband struggled to have his labours published in his Country and could not; and I have struggled to sell his forty years of labour and cannot."

It would take a year to raise the funds needed to acquire Audubon's remarkable drawings. In June of 1863, the Historical Society finally purchased 430 drawings for Audubon's *Birds of America*, along with thirty-four other works. Audubon's drawings have been a highlight of the collection ever since, and holdings in Audubon-related material have grown over time to become the world's largest. The Historical Society now counts in its collection oil paintings, miniatures, and watercolors, as well as the artist's own copy of *The Birds of America* and four copper engraving plates used to produce it, Audubon's life and death masks, and even clippings of his hair and whiskers.

John James Audubon's original watercolor of CAROLINA PARAKEETS, *from about 1825. Purchased for the Society by public subscription from Mrs. John J. Audubon, 1863.17.26*

THE CONSUMMATION OF EMPIRE, *from 1835-36,
the third in Thomas Cole's epic five-canvas allegory of a
young civilization, doomed to suffer the fate of Old World
empires. New-York Gallery of the Fine Arts, 1858.3*

NEGRO LIFE AT THE SOUTH (OLD KENTUCKY HOME) *of 1859, a masterful portrait of the African American experience by Eastman Johnson. The Robert L. Stuart Collection, on permanent loan from the New York Public Library, 1944, S-225*

A Retreat into Nature

ASHER B. DURAND (1796-1886) built a career out of painting the lush scenery of the Hudson River Valley, the Catskills, the Adirondacks, and the White Mountains. Although this may not sound like an unusual accomplishment today, it was a rather exceptional feat during the mid-nineteenth century. Since colonial times, New York's painters had relied on portraiture to support themselves, responding to a steady demand among the city's wealthy, status-conscious merchant class for their commissions.

The emergence of landscape painting as a respectable genre demanded a different type of patron, however, and a new form of appreciation for the finished work of art.

Durand's romantic landscapes, like his 1844 *The Solitary Oak,* offered the merchants and financiers who commissioned them a glimpse of nothing less than the Divine in nature, revealing the redemptive power of the American country-side. His bucolic images of rural life in the East presented easily graspable subject matter to a

new class of patrons, unversed in the esoteric theories of European art. His *Solitary Oak* presents a view of the wilderness, penetrated by civilization: an opulent and plentiful agrarian scene, with a working farm, well-fed cattle in repose beneath an ancient oak tree, and a view of the expansive landscape in the distance. As a critic for the *New Mirror* noted, "it seemed...as if that landscape alone would be a retreat, a seclusion, a world by itself to retreat into from care or sad thoughts—so mellow and deep was the distance, so true to nature the colouring the drawing, so sweetly poetical the composition."

Yet Durand's painting is not as simple as it seems. As historians have noted, this image of the American landscape celebrates a way of life that was quickly vanishing at the time. Land speculation and industrial progress were transforming rural America, a fact Durand undoubtedly knew. If in *The Solitary Oak* these forces are rendered obliquely, it is because the painter consciously chose to emphasize something else. Durand wrote eloquently about his belief that the merchant class propelling the industrial revolution would benefit from a return to the innocent, natural setting of childhood, and his paintings offer a means of doing just that. His views of the American countryside as a symbol of divine promise were designed to comfort a patron class, responsible—at least in part—for bringing about vast physical and cultural changes in the American landscape.

In 1845, Durand donated *The Solitary Oak* to the New-York Gallery of the Fine Arts, the first permanent public art gallery in New York. In 1858, the contents of the gallery, which included fourteen additional works by Durand, were given to the New-York Historical Society. Other works by the artist followed. At the time of Durand's death, the society purchased the contents of his studio, which included a desk, a small sofa, and a carrying case that still contained two canvases rolled up inside. A large collection of Durand's work came to the Historical Society between 1903 and 1935, through the artist's descendants. Today, the society is the single greatest repository of Durand-related material in the world, housing not only landscape paintings, but also a vast array of portraits, historical and genre scenes, drawings, studies from nature, and sketchbooks executed by the artist.

Asher B. Durand's lyrical landscape, The Solitary Oak (The Old Oak), *of 1844. New-York Gallery of the Fine Arts, 1858.75*

The 360-Degree Experience

THIS DETAILED PANORAMA of New York City, drawn in eight sections, is thirteen inches high and an impressive twenty feet long. When arranged in a circle, it shows the city as it appeared between 1842 and 1845 from the steeple of the North Dutch Church, which stood at the northwest corner of Fulton and William streets. Edward Burckhardt (1815-1903), the son of a Swiss ribbon manufacturer, created this panorama in the tradition of European landscape painting of the late-eighteenth century, which attempted to record the experience of viewing the natural landscape or city skyline in a full 360 degrees.

In a period before airplane travel, viewing the world in this way was a novel experience. Travelers on the Grand Tour climbed mountains and cathedral towers all over Europe to take in the panoramic view of the surrounding landscape. Circular painting developed as a means of capturing the tourist's experience of those often-spectacular vistas. Artists created records of the places they visited to keep as visual souvenirs. Some travelers paid artists to accompany them and record their impressions, while others, unencumbered by academic theories of "correct" perspective, created similar views for themselves, by simply sketching what they saw.

Burckhardt was not an artist by profession, but a businessman. He came to New York in 1839, and when he drew this panorama, the great mid-century economics boom was just getting started. Guidebooks to New York published in the ensuing decade included views like Burckhardt's as a means of helping visitors grasp the city in its entirety. By this time, New

Detail of Edward Burckhardt's PANORAMIC VIEW OF NEW YORK CITY, *illustrating mid-nineteenth century urban sprawl making its way up the island of Manhattan. Gift of Mrs. Harold Farquhar Hadden, 1915.76*

York had become the most densely populated city in the country, boastful of its emerging metropolitan status, grandeur, and sheer scale. Its inhabitants had made their way uptown, "above Bleecker," to Union and Washington Squares, and would soon populate Madison Square and Gramercy Park. When Burckhardt left New York for London in 1870, the open lands shown in his view beyond City Hall to the northwest had been developed and inhabited.

The centuries-old urge to view the landscape from the highest possible point still persists today. Although the steeple of the North Dutch Church disappeared long ago, the observation decks of the Empire State Building and the World Trade Center attract thousands of sightseers daily.

Photograph, looking toward the Upper West Side from City Hall, about 1890. Print Room, Geographic Files #51228

Good Help Was Hard to Find

THE SCENE IS an intelligence office, or employment agency, for female domestic servants. Several women huddle together on a bench, having responded to an advertisement in the *Sun*, a copy of which lies on the floor. An employer calmly assesses two potential candidates: one faces the viewer, while the other looks at the employment agent, a well-dressed man in the center of the room. He gestures toward the client as if to ask, "Well, who will it be?"

The painter of this genre scene, William Henry Burr (1819-1908), did more than simply record events in this scene; in *The Intelligence Office*, he created one of the only sympathetic images of female domestic servants painted in the mid-nineteenth century. Burr highlights the heads of the two women searching for work, for example, but hides the face of the wealthy employer in shadow. He creates a gaping space between the potential servants and the soon-to-be served, suggesting an unbreachable social divide. Between the two the artist places the employment agent, his uninterested expression and open palm raising doubts about the pledge of honesty that hangs above his head. By the look of resignation on the applicant's face, turned toward the viewer, Burr clearly communicates his sympathy for this young woman; clasping her cloak across her breast, she is poised to descend into a life of drudgery and perhaps even degradation.

In 1849—the year Burr executed the painting—the climate of popular opinion was against the artist. His work failed to inspire pity for the plight of his subjects among his upper-class audience. Negative views toward domestics were widespread. Good help was literally hard to find, especially in densely populated cities. As native-born women began leaving domestic service for jobs in mills and factories, unskilled immigrants from Ireland and Germany took their place. Ethnic and religious differences widened the gap between employer and employed. The ethical standards of intelligence offices deteriorated, as unscrupulous agents exploited their clients by over-registering servants and setting exorbitant placement fees. At mid-century, the patrons—not the domestic workers—were more often perceived as the victims of this system.

This may help explain why Burr's sympathetic view of the "servant problem" didn't sell.

> *"Those offices which profess to recommended domestics, are 'bosh,–nothing.' In nine cases out of ten, the keepers are in league with the servants; and in the tenth, ignorance, dishonesty, or carelessness will prevent any benefit resulting from their 'intelligence.' All that you can do is, to take the most decent creature who applies; trust in Providence, and lock everything up."*
>
> —Anonymous Etiquette Manual, 1836

When this painting was exhibited at the National Academy of Design in 1849, it was neither purchased nor reviewed. Genteel patrons were perhaps no more willing to bring a reminder of such a distasteful experience into their homes than critics were willing to admit such a topic into the repertoire of American

THE INTELLIGENCE OFFICE *of 1849, William Henry Burr's poignant commentary on the ethics of domestic employment agencies. Purchased by the Society, 1959.46*

painting. For the time being, Americans turned a blind eye not only to the fact that the lower classes existed in the United States, but also that the American domestic ideal rested upon their exploitation. After executing a few more genre scenes, Burr gave up painting altogether and pursued other outlets for his social commentary, working as a court reporter and publishing a number of moral tracts.

Arctic Adventures

ON MAY 25, 1845, the seasoned arctic explorer Sir John Franklin embarked from his native England on an expedition to the North Pole. Spotted in the upper waters of Baffin's Bay a year later, he was never seen nor heard from again.

The plight of Franklin and his crew aroused the sympathies of people everywhere, as repeated efforts to rescue them from the Arctic failed. In 1850, New York merchant Henry Grinnell loaned two of his vessels to the U.S. Navy to aid in the search. Elisha Kent Kane, M.D. (1820-1857), the physician and naval officer featured in this painting, joined the

Posthumous portrait of ELISHA KENT KANE, M.D., *painted by Thomas Hicks in 1858 with the aid of photographs and engravings. Gift of several ladies of New York, 1859.1*

expedition as surgeon and naturalist. Armed with a stock of coarse woolen clothing, a wolf-skin robe, and a few books, Kane boarded Grinnell's *Advance* at the Brooklyn Navy Yard along with other officers and volunteer seamen.

The expedition lasted sixteen months and resulted in the discovery of Franklin's first winter camp. Kane led a second expedition on the *Advance* in 1853. Although it, too, was unsuccessful in locating Franklin, Kane and his men collected valuable geographic, meteorological, and geologic data from the Arctic. Running low on supplies, they abandoned their icebound ship and traveled overland to reach a settlement in Greenland. After eighty-three days, they were rescued by a relief expedition and returned to New York City in October of 1855 as heroes.

Public fascination with the North Pole increased each time new information about this uncharted territory was released. Kane published accounts of his harrowing journeys in 1853 and

1856; based on his personal journal entries, his books catered to the nation's growing appetite for tales of Arctic exploration, and armchair explorers devoured them. By 1857—the year of Kane's untimely death—the details of his life had become the stuff of national legend.

This posthumous portrait, painted in 1858 by the popular artist Thomas Hicks (1823-1890), shows the celebrated explorer seated in a ship's cabin and surrounded by charts, navigational instruments, and a globe—the tools of his trade. Although the painter may have invented these details, he rendered his subject's facial features with remarkable accuracy, most likely copying them from an earlier portrait or photograph of Kane.

A Nightingale Sang

BUILT BETWEEN 1807 and 1811, this circular fort has a long and varied history. Located at the southern tip of Manhattan one hundred yards off shore, Fort Clinton was built to protect New York Harbor from invasion by the British. It would subsequently serve as an immigration station, an aquarium, a national monument, and a ticket booth for ferries to the Statue of Liberty and Ellis Island. But one of the most memorable periods in the structure's history was between 1823 and 1855, when the city of New York allowed entrepreneurs to convert the fort into Castle Garden, a concert hall and center for popular entertainments. This view of Castle Garden commemorates a landmark event in the history of the performing arts in New York, which took place there in 1850—the first American performance of the "Swedish Nightingale," Jenny Lind.

By mid-century, Johanna Maria Lind (1820-1887) was known throughout Europe as the leading contralto-soprano. She was virtually unknown to American audiences, however, until the showman P. T. Barnum staked his career on bringing her to New York. Barnum had never seen Lind, nor heard her sing, but acting on the strength of her reputation in Europe, he mortgaged everything he owned, borrowed an additional five thousand dollars, and paid the singer $187,500 in advance for a two-year, one-hundred-and-fifty-concert tour.

Lind's debut was brilliantly managed, a tour-de-force in entertainment promotion. Barnum's well-placed newspaper articles and publicity stunts aroused the interest of a public unaccustomed to attending world-class musical performances. The Great Jenny Lind Opening Concert Ticket Auction, for example, fetched $224 for the privilege of purchasing the first ticket to Lind's American premiere. For that performance, Barnum rented the largest concert hall in New York City—Castle Garden—and on the evening of September 11, 1850, the singer opened to a capacity crowd of seven thousand. Thanks in large part to Barnum, Jenny Lind's United States debut was an unparalleled popular and critical success.

Jasper Francis Cropsey (1823-1900)—one of the best-known, second-generation members of the Hudson River School—painted a view of Castle Garden for Lind as a souvenir of her spectacular performance. He created another view—this romantic, moonlit version—in 1859, while living in London, four years after Castle Garden had been converted to other uses. Both paintings are housed in the Luce Center. They not only commemorate Lind's inaugural performance in America, but also document a brief but illustrious phase in the site's history.

Jasper Francis Cropsey's moonlit view of CASTLE GARDEN, *the site of Jenny Lind's spectacular American debut in 1850. Purchased by the Society, 1972.13*

Monuments to a Noble Race

IN THE WINTER of 1822, George Catlin (1796-1872) encountered a delegation of Native Americans from the West trading in the streets of Philadelphia and from that time on devoted his life to recording their distinctive ways of life. Between 1824 and 1829, the artist executed portraits of native people living on their reservations in upstate New York, and in 1830 he moved to the frontier city of St. Louis to paint the Plains tribes in their "natural state." Catlin made five trips along the Mississippi and Missouri rivers and throughout the Great Plains, creating countless field sketches and painting more than 450 portraits and landscape scenes, all designed to rescue "from oblivion the looks and customs of the vanishing races of native men in America."

Welcomed by tribes throughout North America, Catlin witnessed events that no other white man had ever been allowed to see. He made as accurate a visual record of his observations as possible and took copious notes on the tribes' religious practices, ceremonies, laws, moral codes, and games. Catlin created a one-of-a-kind visual and literary account that preserves many intimate and ceremonial aspects of Native American life in the 1830s.

In this drawing, *Blackfoot Doctor (a Medicine Man)*, Catlin documents a custom of the Blackfoot, a nomadic tribe of the northwestern plains. Like

BLACKFOOT DOCTOR (A MEDICINE MAN), *a vivid image of a Native American ritual, witnessed by George Catlin in the 1830s and drawn from memory over thirty years later. Purchased from George Catlin, 1872.23.173*

many Native American tribes, the Blackfoot relied upon the supernatural powers of a medicine man—a combination physician and high priest—to cure illness. Here, Catlin depicts the Blackfoot medicine man's last attempt to save the life of a great warrior, who has been shot twice in the chest by a rival tribesman. Catlin witnessed this event at the mouth of Yellowstone in 1832 and wrote about it in his 1841 book, *Letters and Notes on the Manners, Customs, and Conditions of the North American Indians*, calling it a tragedy of "the most grotesque character" he had ever seen. Before a thousand villagers, Catlin recalls, the medicine man—dressed in ceremonial regalia, with rattle in one hand and a medicine spear in the other—snarled and growled like a grizzly bear in incantations of the Good and Bad spirits. As the wounded man cried out in pain, the doctor danced around him, jumped over him, pawed at him, and rolled him on the ground. After a half-hour, the unfortunate warrior died.

The medicine man's ceremonial costume was made from the skin of a yellow bear; a great rarity in the area, it was thought to have magical powers. The outfit became part of a vast collection of artifacts that Catlin assembled and exhibited in his Indian Gallery, alongside his portraits of the Plains people. The gallery opened in September of 1837 in New York City to packed audiences and rave reviews, and the collection went on to similar triumphs in other great cities throughout America and Europe. When interest in Native American culture waned due to over-saturation, so did Catlin's fortune. After a brief stay in debtors' prison, the artist was bailed out by a wealthy American, who took the contents of his Indian Gallery as collateral. The image of the Blackfoot medicine man forms part of a collection of outline drawings which Catlin executed from memory, in an attempt to recreate his life's work.

The outlines, drawn between 1866 and 1868 when Catlin was living in Brussels, Belgium, were intended for a subscription

> *"I have, for many years past, contemplated the noble race of red men who are now spread over these trackless forests and boundless prairies, melting away at the approach of civilization…and I have flown to their rescue…[that], phoenix-like, they may rise from the 'strain on a painter's palette,' and live again upon canvas…the living monuments of a noble race."*
>
> —George Catlin, 1841

volume that was never produced. Instead, 220 of the 221 original graphite-and-ink drawings were purchased at the time of his death by the New-York Historical Society, where Catlin had been a member. An irreplaceable historical and ethnographic record of nineteenth-century Native American culture, Catlin's outlines (like his original paintings and artifacts, now in the Smithsonian) preserve the looks and customs of the trans-Mississippi tribes for all time.

Imaging America's Antiquity

FREDERIC EDWIN CHURCH (1826-1900) never had the benefit of European training, considered essential for success in the art world of nineteenth-century America. He did, however, have the privilege of working with artist Thomas Cole (1801-1848), the celebrated founder of the Hudson River School style of painting. From 1844 to 1848, Church lived in Catskill, New York, and studied with Cole, who taught him to view landscape painting as a means for expressing noble ideas. Following Cole's example, Church depicted nature as a reflection of divine creation, transforming the terrain of the Hudson River Valley, the Berkshires, the Catskills, and the Green Mountains into profound moral landscapes.

Church left Catskill for New York City in 1848, and within two years his paintings took on a decidedly new character. Church became fascinated with the geological forces that contemporary scientists claimed had created the earth, and he began to feature awe-inspiring geological formations in his paintings. His search for subject matter led him to South America, Newfoundland, Labrador, Jamaica, the Near East, and eventually, to Ecuador, where he studied and sketched equatorial volcanoes. In 1858, Church used those carefully drawn field sketches to create *Cayambe*, which entered the Historical Society's collection in 1944.

Church depicts Cayambe, the 19,000-foot peak in the Andes Mountains, at dusk. The sun's setting rays illuminate only the snow-capped volcanic peak, highlighted against a deep blue sky. In the foreground, Church records tropical plants with scientific accuracy; their leaves reflect the ambient light that suffuses the air at twilight. But the foreground of this painting also includes something that Church had not encountered first-hand in Ecuador: the ruins of an ancient civilization. The carved stone column topped by an orb is most likely not based on direct observation, but rather borrowed from a book on Central American antiquities provided by his patron, Robert L. Stuart.

Stuart, a New York City sugar refiner and great patron of American art, had commissioned *Cayambe*. Like the artist, Stuart was a student of natural history, but he also had a passion for archeology. Events relating to the commission suggest that Church added the ancient ruin to his composition after showing a preliminary sketch to his patron. The addition of this detail is unusual for Church, who included several ruins in his paintings of Greece and the Near East, but rarely—if ever—featured them in his South American landscapes.

Why Church included a vestige of ancient American civilization in *Cayambe* is unclear.

Perhaps he painted it simply to please his patron. Public interest in pre-Columbian culture was beginning to peak at mid-century, and travelers to remote regions of the continent were daily discovering the remnants of former civilizations. Whatever its source, the inclusion of the plinth and orb adds an element of human history to the painting—one that complements its theme of natural history. At a time when the relatively young nation was looking to adopt a new myth of national origins, having renounced—at least in theory—its dependence upon Europe, Church's landscape suggests the antiquity of America itself. Just as the volcano in the distance implies pre-historic, geological origins for the continent, the relic hints at the ancient beginnings of an indigenous American civilization.

Frederic Edwin Church's majestic 1858 painting of the volcanic peak CAYAMBE. *The Robert L. Stuart Collection, on permanent loan from the New York Public Library, 1944, S-91*

A Quiet Afternoon on the Shrewsbury River

ON A MIRROR-LIKE expanse of water, which winds its way from the left foreground of this painting to a distant barrier-beach on the right, pleasure boats glide silently under sail. The scene is the North Shrewsbury River, now called the Navesink, a tidal estuary that joins up with the Shrewsbury River and empties into the Atlantic Ocean at New Jersey's Sandy Hook Bay. John Frederick Kensett (1816-1872) painted this landscape in 1859, having visited a small fishing village on the far side of the peninsula some seven years earlier. The last and largest of a series of paintings based on his visit to the area, *Shrewsbury River, New Jersey*, repeats the basic compositional elements used in earlier paintings, but introduces minute

The New-York Historical Society

variations in the brightness of the sky and in the rippling of the water.

Kensett's sensitive rendering of light and atmosphere in the Shrewsbury series later earned his painting style the title "Luminist." His works have a clear, radiant quality that lends a still and timeless aspect to nature. The light-infused canvases present to the viewer a divinely inhabited universe, akin to that described by American Transcendentalists Henry David Thoreau and Ralph Waldo Emerson, in which nature functions as a redemptive force.

Kensett became one of the most successful landscape painters of his day. His canvases appealed to a growing class of wealthy industrialists who shared his faith in the restorative power of the American landscape. Like the artist, his patrons frequently traveled to the Catskill Mountains and the Hudson River Valley to commune with nature and to escape the harsh conditions of the city. When they returned to New York, they could reconnect nature through landscape paintings such as Kensett's, the calm shores and expansive horizons of the works providing a soothing antidote to the ills of urban life.

SHREWSBURY RIVER, NEW JERSEY, *of 1859, one in a series of ruminations on the effects of light and atmosphere by the Luminist painter John Frederick Kensett. The Robert L. Stuart Collection, on permanent loan from the New York Public Library, 1944, S-229*

Patriotic Impressions

THE MATURE WORK of Childe Hassam (1859-1935) has long been recognized as one of the finest expressions of American Impressionism. Hassam became fascinated with the vibrant colors and quick, feathery brushstrokes of the Impressionist style while studying in Paris between 1886 and 1889. When he returned to the United States, he brought this new aesthetic with him and employed it over the next thirty years in his paintings of New York City, captured in all conditions of light and weather. Critics praised his later works, such as his flag paintings, for their powerful emphasis on abstract design, patterning, and flattening of space. By the time Hassam painted *Flags on 57th Street, Winter 1918*, form had almost completely dissolved into strokes of paint on canvas.

But Hassam's flag paintings are important not only for their innovative technique, but also for their content: their overt support of America's involvement in World War I. Throughout the war, the flag of the United States hung alongside those of the allied nations—Britain, France, Japan, Portugal, Belgium, Italy, Cuba, Serbia, Brazil, Romania, and revolutionary Russia—on Fifth Avenue between 23rd and 58th streets. By the end of World War I, one of the country's most famous thoroughfares, Fifth Avenue, renamed the "Avenue of the Allies" in 1918, came to symbolize the nation's unified effort on the home front. In his flag paintings, Hassam pays homage both to the importance of American patriotism at home and to the efforts of the Allied forces abroad.

Hassam created his images of flags between 1916 and 1919, often in response to specific events, campaigns, or celebrations. Following the U.S. entry into World War I in the spring of 1917, Hassam's output increased. The Fourth Liberty Loan Drive, held during the autumn of 1918 to help finance the war, inspired his most concentrated effort, when he created five flag scenes in three weeks.

During the autumn and winter of 1917 to 1918, Hassam began experimenting with new perspectives and surface treatments. In *Flags on 57th Street*, Winter 1918—the only snow scene in the flag series—Hassam moves away from Fifth Avenue and its long, dramatic vista to 57th Street, looking west toward the Sixth Avenue elevated train station. Yet this angled, bird's-eye view, taken from Hassam's studio at 130 West 57th Street, is far from a literal copy of what the artist saw from his window. Hassam manipulated the scene for political and aesthetic reasons, packing his canvas with brightly colored flags, increasing their size, scale, and clarity to emphasize their symbolic meaning.

By the end of the war, Hassam had created almost thirty works depicting the decorated parade route along Fifth Avenue and its intersecting streets. The artist exhibited twenty-three of these as a group for the first time at the Durand-Ruel Gallery on November 15, 1918, in celebration of the four-day-old armistice. Since that time, these compelling works of American Impressionism have served as emblems of patriotic sentiment in the United States during World War I.

Childe Hassam's FLAGS ON 57TH STREET, WINTER 1918, *created in homage to the Allied war effort. Bequest of Julia B. Engel (Mrs. Solton Engel), 1984.68*

Sculpture

With over eight hundred pieces in its arsenal, the New-York Historical Society's sculpture collection includes works by hundreds of different artists, executed in a multitude of styles. Carved in wood or marble, or cast in plaster or bronze, works as diverse as tombstones, life masks, and cigar-store Indians document the full range of representational sculpture in America from the colonial period to the present day.

The earliest pieces contained in the Historical Society's encyclopedic collection were executed by foreign-trained artists—the preeminent sculptors of their day, who received commissions for important public works in America. Whether shipped to America by wealthy New York merchants, or executed on American soil by such famous European sculptors as Jean Antoine Houdon (1741-1828), these works in the neo-classical style captured the look of America's first political leaders and gave expression to their ideals.

The works of these foreign emigrés and visiting artists set precedents for American artists and inspired a generation of sculptors to study abroad in the professional art centers of England and Italy. Although some, like Thomas Crawford (1813-1857), never returned home, examples of their work were transported overseas and are now well-represented in the society's collection.

When a new interest in naturalism emerged in the mid-nineteenth century, it was given expression locally by sculptors Henry Kirke Brown (1814-1886) and John Quincy Adams Ward (1830-1910). These artists led the way in developing American themes and illustrating figures from contemporary American life. Selections of their work entered the collection in the late nineteenth century. Perhaps nowhere were the events and encounters of everyday life captured so literally as in the figural groups of John Rogers (1829-1904). His highly-detailed genre scenes elevated narrative sculpture to a respectable form of cultural expression. Gifts and bequests, many from Rogers's own family members, have made the society's collection of Rogers sculpture and related material the most comprehensive in the United States.

Portraits by distinguished artists such as Jo Davidson (1883-1952) and Malvina Hoffman (1885-1966) represent a continuation into the twentieth century of earlier traditions, whereas the Elie Nadelman Collection of Folk Art brings an entirely different dimension to the Historical Society's collection. Nadelman, a sculptor himself, had traveled up and down the eastern seaboard with his wife, Viola, amassing an enormous collection of folk art. With the purchase of this collection and with continued acquisitions in all stylistic modes, the range and depth of the Historical Society's collection continues to expand, making it one of the most valuable resources for the study of American sculpture today.

A Feel for Character

ON SEPTEMBER 14, 1836, Aaron Burr (1756-1836), former New York Senator and vice president under Thomas Jefferson, but better known as the man who won the duel with Alexander Hamilton (1755/57-1804), died at his home on Staten Island. That evening, recalled Burr's undertaker, O. W. Buell, a "mysterious stranger" who had been lurking around Burr's house for weeks knocked at the door. Upon entering, he cast a single glance at the dead man's face, sat down, opened his carpetbag, appropriated a wash bowl and water pitcher, and—without asking anyone's permission—set to work. Buell explained:

> The secret of his long and patient perseverance was then manifest. He was an artist and had been waiting all those days and nights for just the opportunity that was his at last—the propitious hour directly after death, when a perfect plaster-of-Paris cast of the head and features could be taken before the symptoms of decay made themselves visible.

The practice of creating death masks dates to ancient times, but in the early decades of the nineteenth century the demand for these artifacts grew, due in part to their use by phrenologists. Phrenology, the pseudo-science of analyzing human character by studying the shape of a person's skull, came into vogue in the United States through the efforts of Lorenzo and Orson Squire Fowler, who traveled up and down the East Coast examining the heads of willing subjects. Using the balls of their fingers, the brothers probed the contours of each head for its distinguishing bumps and bulges, all the while delivering an entertaining discourse on the subject's "temperament." If the Fowlers could not gain access to a living person's skull, they were happy to apply their trade to a surrogate, and death masks—a direct impression of the original—were considered ideal.

In 1835, the Fowlers and their partner Samuel Wells opened an office in New York City, complete with examination rooms and a lecture hall. In the spring of the following year they added a museum, in which they exhibited plaster casts of a host of remarkable heads: popular historical figures, famous and infamous, living and dead, including artists, scientists, statesmen, murderers, and thieves. They spent thousands of dollars purchasing busts from other phrenologists and commissioning new works from artists. Burr's death mask

DEATH MASK OF AARON BURR, *cast in plaster for the New York phrenologists Fowler & Wells on September 14, 1836, just hours after Burr's death. Gift of Dr. John E. Stillwell, October 18, 1927, 1927.59*

joined a collection that included George Washington, William Tecumseh Sherman, and Samuel Finley Breese Morse, the inventor of the Morse code. By 1842, with one thousand crania lining the walls, Fowler & Wells' Phrenological Museum had become a New York landmark.

In addition to exhibiting busts, Fowler & Wells offered character analysis of their foremost subjects. In Lydia Maria Child, the author of influential antislavery tracts, they detected the "radical notions" of a woman who "enjoys herself with a book and pen more than in household arrangements." Walt Whitman possessed "sympathy" as well as "indolence and a tendency to the pleasures of voluptuousness." The phrenologists were less flattering to Burr: they described him as "marked by excessive amativeness, destructiveness, combativeness, firmness and large self esteem."

Fowler & Wells' reading perhaps tells us more about the climate of opinion surrounding Burr at the time of his death than it reveals about his actual character. The reputation of this one-time leader of the national anti-Federalist movement had suffered greatly in the years following his vice presidency. By 1836 it was in tatters. His duel with Hamilton thirty-two years earlier—the culmination of long-standing animosity between the two political rivals— marked the beginning of its descent. Charged with Hamilton's murder in both New York and New Jersey, Burr finished his term as vice president but was increasingly marginalized from mainstream politics. Arrested for having hatched a scheme in which the western portion of the United States would secede, he was eventually tried for treason. Although acquitted of the charge, he spent several years in self-imposed exile in Europe before returning to New York in 1812, politically and financially ruined. Fowler & Wells' deductions about Burr's temperament, based on their examination of this death mask, affirmed the traits of a flawed and fallen man.

In recent years, scholars have revisited Burr's anti-Federalist writings. The statesman's reputation has generally improved, leaving us to wonder what modern-day phrenologists might hypothesize if they were to re-examine Burr's death mask today.

Letter from Aaron Burr to Alexander Hamilton dated June 18, 1804, asking for "prompt and unqualified acknowledgment or denial" of Hamilton's involvement in the circulation of slanderous remarks about his character. Manuscript Department, BV Hamilton, Alexander, #73796

Pitting Colony Against King

THE STAMP ACT, passed by the British Parliament in 1765, imposed a tax on American colonists by requiring a stamp on publications and legal documents. The measure was vehemently opposed by the colonists and sparked an argument about "taxation without representation" that escalated tensions between the British and their subjects—tensions that would lead to revolution. The English statesman William Pitt, the Elder (1708-1778), provided a temporary fix for the situation, however, when in 1766, he lobbied Parliament successfully on behalf of the colonists for the Stamp Act's repeal.

To commemorate Pitt's success, the colonists of New York decided to commission a statue of the "Champion of the American Cause in Parliament" from one of England's finest artists—Joseph Wilton (1722-1803), sculptor to His Majesty, George III. The colonial legislature apparently could not justify the expenditure, however, without also honoring the king himself. Hence, two statues were executed simultaneously by Wilton, imported to the colony, and installed in New York City in 1770. The full-sized marble statue of Pitt, dressed in the long robes of a Roman senator and holding a copy of the Magna Carta in his right hand, was placed at the intersection of Wall and William streets. It bore an inscription expressing "the grateful sense the colony of New-York retains of the many eminent services [Pitt] rendered America, particularly in promoting the repeal of the stamp-act." The larger-than-life size gilt-lead statue of King George III sitting atop his horse was modeled after an antique sculpture depicting

Joseph Wilton's statue of WILLIAM PITT, THE ELDER, *from about 1770. Gift of Mr. Simon F. Mackie, 1864.5*

the Roman emperor Marcus Aurelius. It was placed in the center of Bowling Green and inscribed simply with the name of its subject.

A seminal incident in American history not only inspired the creation of these two statues, but also triggered their destruction. On July 9, 1776, the Declaration of Independence was read aloud before each brigade of the Continental Army posted at New York. That evening, a band of excited patriots pulled down the equestrian statue of King George III. After removing its gold leaf, they ferried large pieces of the statue's equally valuable lead over Long Island Sound, loaded it onto wagons, and hauled it some fifty miles north to Litchfield, Connecticut, where it was cast into bullets for the Continental Army.

But not all of the statue's 4,000 pounds of lead made it to Litchfield. On route, the drivers halted at Wilton, Connecticut. While they were imbibing with their fellow patriots, the legend goes, local loyalists stole pieces of the statue off their wagon and hid them in the area. The decapitated head of George III, still crowned with a laurel wreath, made its way back to

England. The tail of the king's horse, now housed in the Luce Center, surfaced in a swamp around 1871. Fragments of the statue continued to re-emerge, some recent finds—made with the help of metal detectors—occasioning interesting legal challenges to American law of possession, or "Finders Keepers" laws.

The statue of William Pitt fared only slightly better. After the British took possession of New York City in the fall of 1776, they decapitated the friend of the colonists and broke off his arms. Thus violated, the statue remained on its pedestal until 1788, when a group of Wall Street proprietors requested its removal to alleviate traffic congestion. In 1864, it was presented to the New-York Historical Society. Like the tail of King George III's horse, the dismembered William Pitt is a potent symbol of the escalating conflicts that led to American independence.

Tail of the Equestrian statue of George III *by Joseph Wilton, from about 1770. Purchased by the Society, 1878.6*

Hail to the Fire Chief

WHEN THE VOLUNTEER Fire Department of New York City built Fireman's Hall in 1854, they ornamented its masonry walls with implements of fire fighting, carved in relief: hooks and ladders, axes, and even a hydrant. But the most potent emblem of the Volunteer Fire Department was the wooden *Fire Chief* installed on the building's roof. Over seven feet tall, holding a megaphone to his lips with one hand and directing his company with the other, this commanding figure must have reassured area residents that help in fighting the next blaze was never very far away.

Fire posed a major threat to life and property in New York from the city's outset. In colonial times, it was considered the duty of every citizen to join the "bucket brigade" when a fire broke out and come to the aid of his neighbor. In the early years of the republic, individuals began organizing into volunteer companies. Men of every social class, ethnic background, and profession—united by a sense of civic responsibility—signed on. Their dangerous task demanded strength, dependability, and, above all, courage. Countless men died or were paralyzed while protecting the lives and property of others. Their sacrifice earned volunteer firefighters the respect and gratitude of their peers. These guardians of public safety quickly became the heroes of early nineteenth-century urban life.

Popular representations of New York's firefighters only enhanced their mystique. Paintings, lithographs, and prints, like those of Currier & Ives, frequently depicted men in the midst of battling tremendous conflagrations. Fire chiefs were prominently featured, often in the same pose as this sculpture, with trumpet pressed to lips. Poems and plays paid tribute to their valor. Newspapers and weekly magazines chronicled outstanding acts of bravery and printed lengthy descriptions of parades and social events sponsored by the companies.

Historians point out that reporters sometimes turned a blind eye to the shortcomings of these volunteers or distorted the truth, perhaps in an attempt to preserve public confidence in the ability of these unchartered companies to control the unpredictable and catastrophic effects of fire.

The image of the volunteer firefighter as an icon of civic virtue came under attack in the early 1860s. Some scholars speculate that their involvement in local politics left New York firefighters especially susceptible to politically motivated criticism. Others point to a change in the social and moral climate of the nation: a new emphasis on paid work and on the family as the anchor of the community may have tarnished the reputations of men idling about a fire station. Still others credit the rise of a professional order, which required the bureaucratic organization of public functions. Whatever the cause, legislation passed in New York on March 30, 1865, established the first full-time, paid municipal fire department in the country.

Rendered obsolete, the volunteers disbanded their companies. They removed the ornaments from their fire houses, trucks, and other equipment and in some cases destroyed or hid them to prevent them from being co-opted by their successors. The carved figure of the *Fire Chief* from Fireman's Hall resurfaced in Paterson, New Jersey, in the 1920s, when Viola and Elie Nadelman discovered it in the cook-loft of an old volunteer firehouse. The folk art collectors purchased it for their personal museum, and in 1937 the New-York Historical Society bought it along with other objects from the Nadelmans' collection.

FIRE CHIEF, *from the roof of Fireman's Hall at 155 Mercer Street, New York City. Purchased from Elie Nadelman, 1937.328*

Nineteenth-century
BABY WALKER.
Inv. 14959

A Lesson in Colonial Child Rearing

THE FORM OF this pine child's walker, derived from the Dutch *loopwagen*, probably originated in Holland or Germany and came to New York in the seventeenth or eighteenth century. What it says about attitudes toward child rearing during that time might be enough to make modern parents blanch.

In Western Europe and the colonies, the qualities that were thought to separate humans from other animals were their abilities to walk erect, speak, and reason. Babies, naturally, could do none of these things. Children—all temper, impulse, bad manners, and mess—were trained as early as possible to enter the sensible, orderly world of adults. Healthy children were expected to walk before their first birthday, and devices like this walker were created to help them to do just that.

Constructed without a seat, the walker was designed to discourage crawling. It fastened securely around the infant's waist, propping him up and leaving him no option but to stand or walk. Walkers provided other benefits as well: they kept babies off of cold, dirty floors and out of harm's way in busy households.

Seventeenth- and eighteenth-century European notions of child rearing were abandoned by some American communities long before they fell out of favor in others. Objects associated with those notions either fell into disuse or were adapted to conform with changing ideas about childhood. A version of the *loopwagen* has endured into the twenty-first century, perhaps because it still gives curious children their first taste of independence. But it exists in modified form: today's walkers are made out of plastic and are equipped with a seat, so that children can rest their weary legs.

Public Fashion, Private Tradition

WHEN JANE KETELTAS (1734-1817) married James Beekman (1732-1807) in 1752, she probably brought this chest into their home as part of her dowry. The massive walnut kas (from the Dutch word *kast*, meaning cupboard or wardrobe) was made in the Netherlands during the late-seventeenth century and most likely sailed with Jane's maternal ancestors to New Amsterdam. Dutch women were entitled by law to inherit and bequeath property, and kasten—along with the fine linens they often contained—were considered valuable assets. Although English law abolished dowries in 1664, colonial Dutch women carried on this tradition well into the next century.

Over seven feet tall and six feet wide, this kas is ornamented with bold moldings and elaborately carved scrolls and shields. Kasten were status symbols for the Dutch middle class, which may help explain why Dutch settlers went through the trouble and expense of importing such enormous pieces of furniture to the colonies. James Beekman, a successful dry goods merchant of Dutch ancestry, was part of the emerging Dutch middle class in New York, and the historical significance of owning such an important piece of furniture would not have been lost on him or his peers.

Around the time of Beekman's marriage to Keteltas, however, the popularity of the kas began to wane in Europe and the colonies, eclipsed by the introduction of the English high chest and other forms of storage, such as built-in cupboards and closets. Beds were moved out of eighteenth-century parlors and into more private chambers, and kasten frequently went with them.

These changes in fashion were most likely important to the Beekmans. Like other members of their social class, they probably followed popular European taste. When the Beekmans moved from the North Ward—a working-class neighborhood filled with Dutch immigrants—to the more stylish Queen Street, and finally in 1763, to Mount Pleasant, their country estate, records indicate that they outfitted their home with rococo gaming tables, dining tables, tea tables, and all their attendant accessories—the stylish furnishings of the day.

Although Jane and James Beekman may have moved the kas to a less prominent area, they retained the piece as part of their household furnishings. A vital link to the Beekmans' shared Dutch ancestry, the kas descended through the family until 1941, when Dr. Fenwick Beekman presented it to the New-York Historical Society.

A seven-foot-tall KAS, *brought to New York from the Netherlands. Gift of Dr. Fenwick Beekman, 1941.914*

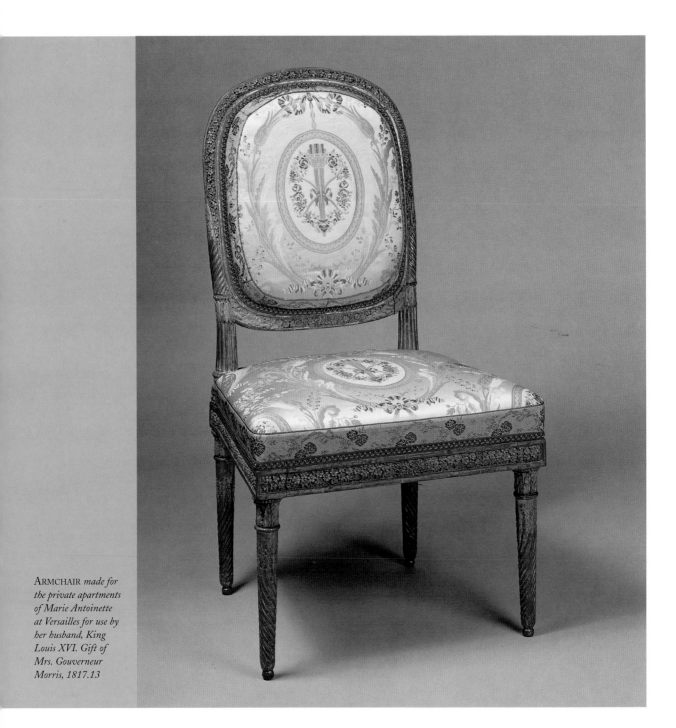

ARMCHAIR *made for the private apartments of Marie Antoinette at Versailles for use by her husband, King Louis XVI. Gift of Mrs. Gouverneur Morris, 1817.13*

A Chair for the King

THE FIRST PIECE of furniture acquired by the New-York Historical Society was literally fit for a king. This eighteenth-century French side chair, purchased by Gouverneur Morris and donated by his widow in 1817, was originally part of a fourteen-piece suite created for Marie

Antoinette's *grand cabinet interieur*, or private apartments, at Versailles.

Gouverneur Morris (1752-1816), one of the founders of the American Republic, served as U.S. Minister to the embattled French court between 1792 and 1794. He was one of many

American statesmen grateful to France for its help during the American Revolution and sympathetic to the plight of King Louis XVI and Marie Antoinette through the years leading up to the French Revolution. Morris was so sympathetic, in fact, that some say he devised an escape plan for the king and queen at the height of the Terror.

Morris's diaries show an enthusiastic interest in French wine, French women, and French furniture. A man of sophisticated tastes, he became one of the first great collectors of French decorative arts in America. After Louis XVI and his queen were stripped of their power and executed in 1793, the possessions from their royal estate at Versailles were auctioned off to the public. Morris bought several pieces from a suite of furniture originally created for Marie Antoinette's private apartment, including this chair, which was designed to seat the king.

Morris returned to New York in 1798, where the chair became part of the furnishings for his country estate, Morrisania. In 1804 he joined other prominent New Yorkers in founding the Historical Society. He served as the organization's vice president between 1810 and 1815 and then as its president until his death in 1816. Mrs. Gouverneur Morris donated the chair to the Historical Society one year later, "for the President of the Society's seat."

The French armchair was made in the royal furniture manufactory in 1779. It was designed by Jacques Gondoin (1737-1818), architect and designer of furniture to the French crown, and constructed by François II Foliot (1748-about 1786), one of the eighteenth century's most talented craftsmen. Remnants of fabric found on the chair indicate that it was originally upholstered in an intricate white silk weave, enriched with elaborate braid and tassels. The upholstery was by far the most expensive item in the suite. The royal inventory number 194 and the crowned *W* of the Chateau of Versailles are stenciled on the webbing of the chair's original seat. An entry in the *Journal du Garde-Meuble* confirms that the chair was delivered to Versailles on October 20, 1779, and that it was explicitly designated for use by King Louis XVI—the only piece in the suite to bear this distinction.

At some point after entering the Historical Society's collection, the chair was placed in a New Jersey storage facility. It was rediscovered in 1985, when the institution initiated a conservation plan for all of its collections. Over the years, layers of soot had accumulated in the intricate carving on the chair's frame, its delicate upholstery had disintegrated, and the gesso and gilding on its front legs had come loose. The stabilization and restoration of the king's chair was begun, with grants from the J. Paul Getty and Florence Gould foundations.

The Historical Society hired a conservator in Paris to clean the chair's frame, repair its joinery, and removed successive layers of its gilding. Gaps in the carved surface decoration were patched and sculpted in keeping with the original spirit of the piece. After careful analysis of the chair's original finish, new gilding was applied using an eighteenth-century formula of rabbit-skin glue, essence of beef spleen, and twenty-three karat gold leaf. During a second phase of conservation, the original upholstery, horsehair stuffing, and webbing were carefully removed; they are now housed in the Luce Center, but kept in a cabinet away from damaging effects of light. A new seat was fashioned, covered with reproduction fabric, and set in place. The conservation of the chair restores the object to it original grandeur, while preserving as much of its original substance and multi-layered history as possible.

French royal inventory number and crowned "W" of Versailles, stenciled on the underside of the chair's original seat. Conservation Files, Condition Photographs

Patterns of Taste in Colonial Cabinetmaking

ONE OF ONLY two known pieces of furniture of this form made in America, this lady's dressing table—built to the specifications of master English furniture designer Thomas Sheraton (1751-1806)—illustrates how American craftsmen used imported pattern books to reproduce popular English designs. Cabinetmakers throughout Europe and America coveted pattern books, which illustrated the most sought-after designs. By the end of the eighteenth century, pattern books like Sheraton's reached America, becoming invaluable to cabinetmakers who catered to the wealthy merchant class and their taste for the latest European trends. The design for this dressing table appeared in Sheraton's *Cabinet Maker's and Upholsterer's Drawing Book*, published in London in 1793.

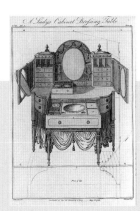

Plate 49 of Sheraton's 1793 CABINET MAKER'S AND UPHOLSTERER'S DRAWING BOOK, *Library Collections, #73196*

Made between 1795 and 1810, this dressing table was purchased by Robert L. Livingston (1775-1843), presumably for his wife, Margaret Maria Livingston (1783-1818). The distant cousins married in 1798 and between 1801 and 1805, lived in Paris with Margaret's father, Chancellor Robert R. Livingston, who was then serving as minister to France. There, the couple was no doubt exposed to the finest in English and Continental tastes by the chancellor, one of America's earliest patrons of the arts. After returning from France, the two lived at Clermont, the Livingston family's Hudson Valley estate, which Margaret inherited in 1813, upon her father's death. Whether this particular piece was used at Clermont is not known for certain, but the Historical Society acquired it and other pieces of refined, English-style furniture from Livingston's descendants in 1951.

American craftsmen followed English prototypes with varying degrees of accuracy, depending on their skill, the availability of materials, and the preferences of their clients. This mahogany cabinet dressing table faithfully reproduces Sheraton's design. Its two cabinets flank an oval mirror placed above two small drawers. The cabinet doors have inset oval mirrors and enclose banks of drawers and pigeonholes. Along with a leather writing surface and compartments for ink and sand (used to blot wet ink), the lower section of the dressing table contains additional drawers and a circular cutout designed to hold a wash basin. According to Sheraton's patternbook, the dressing table contained "every requisite for a lady to dress at."

DRESSING TABLE, *made in New York after a design by English cabinetmaker Thomas Sheraton. Gift of Goodhue Livingston, Sr. Inv. 14982*

A French Revolution in Furniture Design

NEW YORK CITY emerged during the Federal period as the leading center for furniture production on America's eastern seaboard. Although New York had long been a magnet for craftsmen from Europe and from elsewhere in America, the French Revolution set off a wave of immigration that changed the history of furniture making in the city. Between 1799 and 1820, a large number of French tradesmen fled the turmoil of their homeland and settled in New York. These highly skilled cabinetmakers, chairmakers, carvers, joiners, turners, gilders, and upholsterers forged a direct link between French and American furniture making traditions.

Among these immigrants was Charles-Honoré Lannuier (1779-1819). After training as a cabinetmaker in Paris, Lannuier sailed for New York City in 1803. He established himself in the center of the city's furniture-making district, with a shop and warehouse at 60 Broad Street—the former workspace of another talented immigrant, the illustrious Scottish furniture maker Duncan Phyfe. Lannuier lived above his shop, like other craftsmen of his day, renting out additional space to a fellow Frenchman for a mahogany lumberyard. This proved convenient for the cabinetmaker, given his preference for mahogany and other exotic woods, which also happened to appeal to a wealthy clientele. Lannuier became a leading producer of fashionable furniture in the city, setting the standard for furniture in the French Empire style. His winged figures and caryatids and imported French mounts attracted New York's most distinguished patrons, including the Morrises, Van Rensselaers, Stuyvesants, Pierreponts, and Pearsalls. Lannuier died a wealthy man in 1819.

During his lifetime, Lannuier was considered Duncan Phyfe's most gifted competitor. In fact, Lannuier's work was frequently mistaken for Phyfe's, as was the case with this French clothes press. The press is thought to have belonged to Garret Byvanck Abeel (1768-1829), a successful iron and hardware merchant, and his wife Catherine Manchalk (d. 1832). The Abeels presumably used the brass hooks located behind the wardrobe's full-length doors to hang up their coats and dressing gowns. The press remained in the Abeel family for many years, passing first to John Howard Abeel and subsequently to his granddaughter Emeline Abeel Wheeler. Mrs. Wheeler gave it to the society in 1943, believing it to be the work of Duncan Phyfe. The true maker of the piece was only properly identified some twenty years later, after Lannuier's signature was inadvertently discovered on the underside of the plaster bust, located within the cabinet's broken pediment.

FRENCH PRESS, *made in New York by French immigrant Charles-Honoré Lannuier, 1812-19. Gift of Mrs. William Hyde Wheeler, 1943.368*

A Capital Moment in New York's History

FOR A BRIEF but memorable moment in its history, New York City served as the capital of the United States. The Congress of the United States, organized under the Articles of Confederation, moved to New York City in January of 1785 and took up residence in City Hall, alongside New York's municipal government. In the fall of 1788, the city decided to dedicate the entire building to the purposes of the first U.S. Congress, which would begin meeting there in the spring of 1789, following the inauguration of the nation's first president.

The task of transforming City Hall into Federal Hall was entrusted to engineer Pierre-Charles L'Enfant (1754-1825), a French-born architect and engineer who had fought for the colonists during the American Revolution. In just six months, L'Enfant redesigned the 1699 structure built by Dutch settlers and adorned it with an elaborate decorative scheme of stars and stripes. The completed project, rumored to cost some sixty-five thousand dollars, received high praise: the *Gazette* pronounced Federal Hall "on the whole superior to any building in America," and the Common Council of New York proclaimed it "a signal Ornament of this city and a Monument of the Munificance of the Citizens."

The building's facade was decorated with an elaborate wrought-iron balustrade, which incorporates thirteen arrows, one for each state in the new republic. The railing stood in front of a twelve-foot gallery, located under the building's central portico. There, on April 30, 1789, before Congress and a large assembly of citizens, Chancellor Robert R. Livingston (1746-1813) administered the oath of office to George Washington (1732-1799).

New York's tenure as capital was short-lived: Congress left for Philadelphia less than a year after the completion of Federal Hall and, with the help of L'Enfant, began making plans for their new quarters in Washington, D.C. By 1812, New York's Federal Hall had fallen into disrepair. In light of its patriotic associations, the balustrade was removed and incorporated into the design of a new municipal project, Bellevue Hospital. In 1884 it was presented for safekeeping to the Historical Society by the New York City Chamber of Commerce, along with a piece of sandstone upon which Washington stood while being sworn in as president.

Between 1790 and 1812, the building that served as Federal Hall housed a diverse group of tenants, among them the New-York Historical Society. In 1809, founding member John Pintard (1759-1844) came upon six semicircular tables used by Congress, still stored in the structure. He petitioned the Common Council for use of the tables, and they agreed. In 1837, two of the tables joined the Historical Society's collection, along with two pedestal desks, four armchairs, and two console tables

ARMCHAIR, *used by President George Washington during his inauguration in 1789. Gift of Edmund B. Southwick, 1916.7*

RAILING *from New York City's Federal Hall, the site of Washington's presidential inauguration.*
Gift of the Chamber of Commerce of the State of New York, 1884.3

from the House and Senate chambers. The society added to this collection in 1958, when it purchased a speaker's desk and lectern also used by the first U. S. Congress at Federal Hall.

Perhaps the most distinguished piece of Federal Hall furniture entered the collection in 1916. Part of a large set of chairs made in New York City between 1785 and 1789 and used by the Senate, this particular piece achieved relic status when it was appropriated by George Washington during his presidential inauguration. According to tradition, in the minutes before his public swearing-in, Washington mingled with his colleagues in the Senate Chamber. He sat in this chair, with soon-to-be Vice-President John Adams at his side, until it was time to greet the crowds from the gallery outside and receive the oath of office. After the ceremony, he returned to this seat.

A U.S. Marshall for New York's Southern District, William Coventry Waddell, rescued Washington's inaugural chair from oblivion in 1831, after discovering it in a courtroom in New

York's new City Hall. Employees identified the chair as the one used by Washington at his inauguration, and Waddell, recognizing its value as an artifact of the early republic, removed it from the courtroom. He and his family guarded it for over fifty years. They lent it to Ulysses S. Grant in 1873 and James A. Garfield in 1881 for use at their inaugurations who—no doubt cognizant of the wave of nostalgia sweeping over the country in the decades following the Civil War—attempted to benefit politically from the chair's historical association with the nation's most universally adored president. The chair was also used by President Harrison in 1889, at the recreation of Washington's oath-taking in New York City. An enduring symbol of national and local pride, Washington's inaugural chair was happily accepted by the Historical Society from Waddell's heirs.

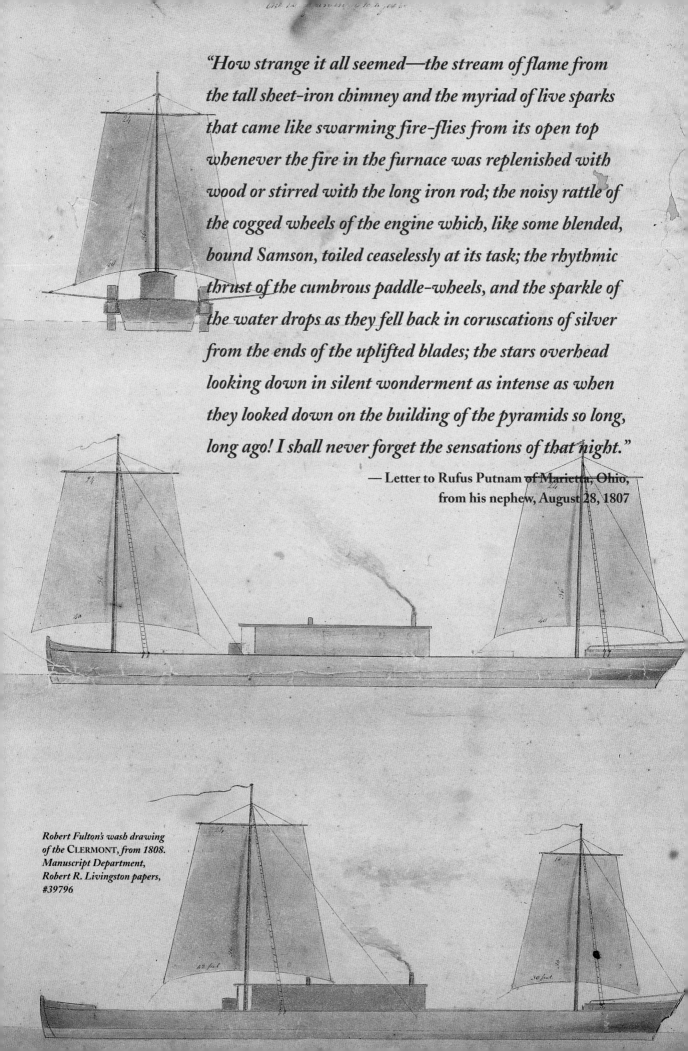

"*How strange it all seemed—the stream of flame from the tall sheet-iron chimney and the myriad of live sparks that came like swarming fire-flies from its open top whenever the fire in the furnace was replenished with wood or stirred with the long iron rod; the noisy rattle of the cogged wheels of the engine which, like some blended, bound Samson, toiled ceaselessly at its task; the rhythmic thrust of the cumbrous paddle-wheels, and the sparkle of the water drops as they fell back in coruscations of silver from the ends of the uplifted blades; the stars overhead looking down in silent wonderment as intense as when they looked down on the building of the pyramids so long, long ago! I shall never forget the sensations of that night.*"*

— Letter to Rufus Putnam of Marietta, Ohio,
from his nephew, August 28, 1807

Robert Fulton's wash drawing of the CLERMONT, from 1808. Manuscript Department, Robert R. Livingston papers, #39796

Full Steam Ahead: Fulton's Clermont

IN 1806, PENNSYLVANIA-born civil engineer Robert Fulton (1765-1815) moved to New York City and set about constructing a full-scale steamboat. The idea of applying steam-power to ships—speeding travel and expanding access to inland waterways—had occurred to many inventors and engineers, but shortages of funds, promotion, and know-how frustrated their efforts. With the skill and advice of shipwright Charles Brownne, and the money and influence of his partner, Chancellor Robert R. Livingston, Fulton built the *Clermont*, a 146-foot long, flat-bottomed vessel with a pair of enormous exposed paddle wheels. Unlike anything ever built before, the *Clermont* became the first steamboat in the United States to successfully navigate the Hudson River.

At one o'clock on August 17, 1807, the *Clermont* set off on her historic maiden voyage. Fulton gave the signal to cast off from Manhattan's western shore, and with a hiss of escaping steam, the exposed water wheels—towering a full seven feet above the deck on either side—began to turn, drenching the passengers and crew. Then the engine stopped, and after about an hour's delay, the *Clermont* was off again. The steamboat moved away from Upper Battery, into the shadows of the Palisades, past Fort Washington. Averaging a speed of four-and-one-half miles per hour, the boat arrived at Tappan Zee just before nightfall.

The *Clermont*'s first passengers spent two nights onboard, arriving in Albany at five o'clock in the evening on August 19. One traveler reported that there were no beds on the boat: passengers slept wrapped in blankets on the cabin floor. By the time commercial service began on the *Clermont* one month later, Fulton had provided furniture. This settee of classic Windsor chair construction, made between 1807 and 1814, is said to have come from the *Clermont*'s cabin.

The settee came into the New-York Historical Society's collection in 1976. It joined an impressive group of material related to Fulton's steamboat enterprise, gathered in 1909 for the centennial celebration of Fulton's first successful trip up the Hudson and the tricentennial of Henry Hudson's first navigation of the river. The Historical Society also owns the *Clermont*'s ship's bell, a gift from the president of the Hudson River Day Line.

By the end of 1812, Fulton was operating six steamboats on the Hudson River, and by 1814, the *Clermont* had been retired, replaced by newer, faster, more efficient models. Traffic on the Hudson reached its peak at mid-century, with steamboats delivering passengers between Albany and New York City in less than half a day. Steamboat travel began to decline in 1851, when the Hudson River Railroad reached Albany, but the steamboat's pace and romance continued to attract artists and sightseers until the mid-twentieth century.

SETTEE, *said to have been used on Fulton's steamboat the Clermont. Gift of Randall J. Le Boeuf, Jr., 1976, Inv. 14952*

A Monument to Washington's Memory

IN MAY OF 1856, one of the oldest houses still standing in New York—the Franklin-Osgood-Clinton Mansion at 3 Cherry Street—was demolished to make way for the extension of the Bowery. The fact that George Washington (1732-1799) had lived there while serving as President, between April of 1789 and February of the following year, wasn't reason enough to save it.

By mid-century, New York City's rapid development into a center of commerce and industry had transformed the city. New buildings and neighborhoods had sprung up where swamps and farmland once existed. Streets had been widened to relieve traffic congestion, and the ever-increasing demands of business had required the construction of new thoroughfares connecting the upper and lower sections of the city. To many New Yorkers of the period, the physical links between New York's past and present seemed to disappear daily. Washington's "modest yet spacious mansion," one newspaper columnist reported, had been replaced by a "magnificent pile of iron" constructed by the ever-expanding book-publishing establishment. The "inevitable laws of human progress," he noted, had "left their mark on every side…. In that pitiless march of improvement which spares in its path no monument of memory, however hallowed, the mansion of Washington was swept away forever."

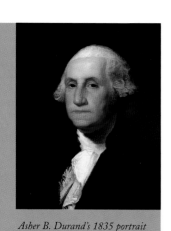

Asher B. Durand's 1835 portrait of GEORGE WASHINGTON. *Gift of the New-York Gallery of the Fine Arts. 1858.32.*

But not quite. Benjamin R. Winthrop (1804-1879) a real estate investor and a member of the New-York Historical Society, happened to pass by the mansion during its demolition and noticed workmen removing its timbers for reuse in other structures. Winthrop rescued a number of the oak beams and commissioned a chair from a local craftsman commemorating the mansion's

presidential history. Designed in the Renaissance Revival style, this monumental armchair is decorated with various political symbols, including the Federal shield and the American Eagle. The oval back panel is flanked by the initials "G" and "W" and is topped by a carved bust of the President himself. On November 3, 1857, Winthrop presented the chair to the New-York Historical Society, the story of its fabrication inscribed on a plaque mounted on the rear seat rail.

During the mid-nineteenth century, "relic wood" like the oak from Washington's home was frequently used to make objects commemorating important people and events in the nation's history. As eyewitnesses to America's struggle for independence passed away, objects such as these grew in value. These "monuments" to the memory of the nation's forefathers seemed to quiet the fear that a period in America's history would be lost forever, and historical societies and museums across the country began acquiring and displaying them.

The design of the chair itself reveals something about how Winthrop valued Washington and his tenure in New York. By combining symbols related to the birth of the republic with the New York City and State coats of arms, Winthrop commemorated Washington as both a national and local hero. In the letter acknowledging Winthrop's gift to the Historical Society, the secretary wrote, "[I]f there is one spot in which the memories that cluster about the career of Washington should be most sacredly and reverently cherished, it is here in New York—the scene of some of his greatest trials and triumphs." By 1857, the chair and other objects associated with Washington's tenure as President in New York had become a source of civic pride—cherished artifacts that helped to define what it meant to be a New Yorker in the mid-nineteenth century.

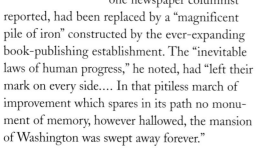

Oak ARMCHAIR, carved from timbers rescued from Washington's home on Cherry Street. Gift of Benjamin Robert Winthrop, 1857.11

Decorative Objects

In 1911, Catharine Augusta De Peyster willed to the New-York Historical Society, along with her collection of family portraits, "articles of household furniture, silverplate and bric-a-brac as may have an interest from their antiquity and associations, some of them having been in the possession of members of my family in the City of New York for upwards of two centuries."

The decorative objects that adorned her home, and those of her ancestors, included porcelain, pottery, silverware, and glass—the focus of this chapter. On view in the Luce Center, these items help visitors imagine what the interiors of New York homes looked like in centuries past. They also tell of the rituals and traditions carried on inside those homes, of the social status and ambitions of their occupants, and of the family relationships sustained there. The stories about artifacts in this collection are as diverse as the materials from which those items are made.

Many of the decorative objects in the Historical Society's collection were assembled by wealthy New York families like the De Peysters. These families had access to the finest goods available to American colonists through the international port of New York; they also had the money and the inclination to purchase them. English and European silver and glass, Chinese export porcelain, and other ceramics began to enter the collection around 1895. Silver and other high-quality goods made locally to compete with imports came in as well. Gifts from the De Peysters were joined by others from the Beekman, Belknap, Livingston, Schuyler, Stuyvesant, and Verplanck families, resulting in

an impressive collection that reflects the tastes of the urban merchant class.

As De Peyster's will suggests, many of these items were prized not only for their antiquity, but also for their associations. Pieces often came to the society with a written record of their passage from generation to generation, or marked with family initials. Some objects were donated or purchased for their association with important local or national events. The society's earliest ceramics acquisition—a plate, received in 1863—was thought by its donor to have been brought to America on the *Mayflower*.

Many of the other decorative objects acquired by the society provide clues about what everyday life was like for the average New Yorker. Household items from upstate New York, purchased in 1922 from Dr. George W. Nash; redware, purchased in 1937 from Elie Nadelman; and pewter, donated by Katharine Prentis Murphy in 1964, all lend different perspectives on the eighteenth- and nineteenth-century experience.

As a result of its early and sustained collecting activity, the Historical Society possesses a remarkable assemblage of decorative objects; in some instances—as in the case of New York silver—the finest in the nation.

A Window on the Past

THESE TWO STAINED-glass windows dating from 1656 are among the earliest artifacts in the New-York Historical Society's collection. They are part of a trio of windows that were given to the society by Mrs. Howard C. Robbins in 1951, three of six heraldic windows she had discovered years earlier in a salvage shop in lower Manhattan.

Robbins purchased the windows just hours after workmen had removed them from a house on Eighth Street slated for demolition. How the windows came to be installed in that house is a mystery. Mrs. Robbins believed that they had "undoubtedly been brought from Holland by a Dutch family and built into their house in New York," but curators now think that they were produced in New Netherlands by a talented Dutch immigrant. Given the scarcity of skilled craftsmen in the colony known to have been capable of producing stained glass, they could only have been made by the illustrious Evert Duyckinck (1621-1702), head of America's first artistic dynasty. In 1638, Duyckinck came to New Netherlands with the Dutch West India Company. Variously described in records of the period as a "limner," "painter," "glazier," "stainer of glass," "painter of glass," "master glazier," and "glass maker," Duyckinck is the only known maker of heraldic windows in New Netherlands at this early date.

During the seventeenth century, heraldic windows adorned the naves of Dutch Reform churches. Wealthy burghers who generously supported their local houses of worship would have their coats of arms painted on glass for display in their church. The names inscribed on the Historical Society's windows link them to the earliest settlers of Albany County. When the first Dutch Reform Church was built there in 1656, these windows, decorated with the armorial bearings of its benefactors, were installed. When a new church was built in 1715, the windows were transferred there, where they stayed until 1806, when that church was demolished. The heraldic windows were removed before the walls of the church came down and given to descendants of the parishioners who had donated them originally.

Before Robbins gave the windows to the Historical Society, she had them installed in her "Dutch house" at Sneden's Landing, built on the Hudson River in the Colonial Revival style. When she moved to California, these windows went with her. How these rare and fragile objects survived their journey—across the country and over time, through five known owners and as many installations— is nothing short of a miracle. Now safely housed in the Luce Center, they not only document an important aspect of seventeenth-century Dutch culture in New Amsterdam, but also shed light on one way in which the value of objects changes over time.

Two STAINED GLASS WINDOWS *by Evert Duyckinck, from 1656. Gift of Mrs. Howard C. Robbins, 1951.414c and 1951.414b*

SILVER BOWL, *made in New York about 1710. Bequest of Catharine Augusta De Peyster, 1911.38*

Marking the Rites of Passage

SOME ARTIFACTS ARE silent about their history; everything we know about them we have learned through historical records about their creator or original owner. Other objects have clues to their history embedded within them, in their form, marks, and inscriptions. This two-handled bowl speaks about its past with a voice of its own.

The maker's mark "W.K/B" in a heart, stamped twice on the lip of the bowl, identifies the bowl's creator as New York silversmith Benjamin Wynkoop (1675-1728). Of Dutch descent, Wynkoop followed the silversmithing traditions of his homeland in this piece, selecting a form and decorative motifs that were typical of Dutch silver. Indeed, only the object's unusually large size and the exuberance of its decoration identify it as a product of New York.

The two handles positioned on opposite sides of the cup point to its use. Following Dutch custom, bowls like this one were filled with brandy and raisins and passed around the dining room table. Guests would help themselves using their own spoons and then hand the bowl off to their neighbor. The small human heads adorning the handles would have helped celebrants steady the bowl by providing convenient thumb-rests.

Brandywine bowls, or *brandewijnskom*, were made in the Netherlands from the mid-seven-teenth century until the nineteenth century. There, they were primarily associated with the *kindermaal*, a gathering of female neighbors held in celebration of the birth of a child. They were also used in ceremonies marking other rites of passage, such as weddings and funerals.

This traditional use of the two-handled bowl is thought to have persisted in Dutch-American households until the nineteenth century. The New-York Historical Society's bowl, from about 1710, may have been made in commemoration of the wedding of its original owners, Cornelius De Peyster (b. 1673) and Mary Bancker De Peyster, which took place in 1694. The couple's conjoined initials, "P/C*M," are marked on one lobe of the bowl. The initials "E.D.P." are engraved on another, and in the bowl's center the name "H.C. de Peyster," written in later script. These names and initials signal the passage of this ceremonial object from one generation of De Peysters to another.

The bowl entered the Historical Society's collection in 1911 through the bequest of Catharine Augusta De Peyster (d. 1911), a descendant of Cornelius and Mary De Peyster. A remarkable artifact from colonial New York, it speaks to the persistence of Dutch tradition within the households of Dutch Americans.

Silver SALVER *presented by Governor William Tryon and the General Assembly of New York to Captain Thomas Sowers, His Majesty's Chief Engineer in America, in 1773. Gift of J. Lawrence Aspinwall, 1928.24*

Rewarding Sowers' Service

THIS IMPRESSIVE SILVER salver was presented to Captain Thomas Sowers, His Majesty's Chief Engineer in America, by Governor William Tryon and the General Assembly of the Province of New York on March 13, 1773. Measuring almost twenty-two inches in diameter and embellished with extraordinary engraving, this salver is a masterpiece of colonial American silver.

The gift recognized Sowers' service in repairing the Battery fortifications on the southern tip of Manhattan Island. Safeguarding this strategic location had been a priority for settlers to this area from the start. Poised at the juncture of the Atlantic Ocean and the Hudson and East rivers, the port of New York was a critical site for the defense of the colonies. Dutch settlers built the first fort there in 1626 (on the site now occupied by the former U.S. Customs House). The English maintained the fort after 1664, adding gun batteries off shore in the eighteenth century. When tensions escalated between loyalists and patriots in 1765, Sowers was first called in to shore up Fort George, the Battery, and the governor's residence, located within the fort. In 1772, after time and bad weather had done further damage to the complex, Governor Tryon recommended additional repairs, and the General Assembly recognized Sowers' aid the following year by presenting him with this showy salver.

Lewis Fueter (1746-1784) was the silversmith responsible for producing this magnificent presentation piece. Born in Switzerland in 1746, his family brought him first to London and then to New York. As a young man, Fueter apprenticed with his father and learned to make the stylish London-influenced silver for which he was known. A staunch loyalist, Lewis Fueter received steady patronage from the royal government and from other loyalists, particularly for military items. His political orientation and excellent silversmithing skills made him a perfect candidate for the job of commemorating the Sowers' service to the crown.

As skillfully crafted as any piece made in London, the salver is raised on hairy-paw feet, each gripping a branch. A large floral wreath surrounds its perimeter. Salvers made excellent presentation pieces, in that their large flat surfaces afforded ample space for engraving and inscriptions. Silversmiths sometimes contracted out services like engraving, and Fueter most likely did so here: sadly, the identity of the engraver of this masterpiece has never been established.

Engraved freehand at the center of the salver is a detailed rendering of the pre-Revolutionary seal of the City of New York. It features a shield with crossed windmill blades, representing one of the principal sources of power in early Manhattan. Within the blades are beavers, which signal the large trade in furs carried on between early Dutch settlers and Native Americans. Flour barrels symbolize another enterprise that brought prosperity to New York. The seal is supported by a sailor on the left, holding a plumb line, and a Native American on the right, holding a bow. Below the seal, implements related to the building and maintenance of fortifications such as a cannon, cannon balls, and barricades are included, in a nod to Sowers' achievements. A banner on a flagstaff is inscribed "GRIII," an overt reference to the recipient's allegiance to George III, King of England.

If the salver's massive size and exquisitely detailed engraving seem somewhat out of scale with the magnitude of Sowers' service, they probably were. In expressing gratitude for Sowers' work on the fortifications, Governor Tryon and the General Assembly were obviously intending to make a public statement. This reward for Sowers' loyalty made palpable the power and prestige of its donor, its recipient, and even craftsmen from whom it was commissioned.

In an ironic twist of fate, Fort George became the stronghold of colonial patriots only three years after His Majesty's Chief Engineer repaired it. The Provincial Congress of New York seized control of the city, declaring royal officials and their supporters enemies of the colonists. While Governor Tryon watched from the safety of a merchant ship anchored in the harbor, the Battery was given up without a fight.

Essential Stoneware

BEFORE THE WIDESPREAD use of refrigerators and mason jars, stoneware vessels were essential equipment in American kitchens, pantries, and cellars. Made from fine-textured gray or tan clay and baked in kilns at high temperatures, stoneware vessels provided durable, impermeable, and easy-to-clean containers for storing and preserving food over time. In the eighteenth and nineteenth centuries they were produced in a limited number of shapes and a wide variety of sizes. Crocks with straight or bulging sides held butter, apple butter, milk, beans, salted meat, or pickles. Cider or vinegar were stored in single-handled jugs with swelling bodies and small mouths that could be corked and sealed. Pitchers held cider, molasses, beer, or ale. Batter pitchers, such as this one, were generally used for keeping and pouring pancake batter.

Functional in purpose, stoneware vessels were usually decorated with only simple, straightforward designs. Stylized flowers, butterflies, and bees, or sometimes animals and patriotic symbols, were carved into the

Stoneware BATTER PITCHER *by Clarkson Crolius, from 1798. Purchased from Elie Nadelman, 1937.587*

damp clay and then filled in with a cobalt blue pigment, which could withstand firing at high temperatures. Craftsmen also painted their pieces in a loose, freehand style, or even stenciled their designs onto the clay. Common salt, tossed into the kiln during the firing process, would vaporize and settle onto the stoneware vessel, creating its characteristic pebbly glaze.

Inscribed by hand around the belly of this vessel are the words, "New York Feby 17th. 1798/Flowered by Clarkson Crolius/Blue." As this inscription suggests, Clarkson Crolius, Sr. (1773-1843), decorated this batter pitcher in 1798. More elaborate in its decoration than most surviving pitchers, it may have been produced as a sample, in order to give potential customers a look at the variety of decorative techniques and patterns from which they could choose. Or, Crolius may have made this piece for some other special purpose, perhaps as a gift for a loved one.

Clarkson Crolius, Sr., was the best-known member of a dynasty of potters that produced stoneware in lower Manhattan for over a century. His great-grandfather, William Crolius (b. 1700) established the family pottery before 1730 at the foot of Pottbaker's Hill, in the vicinity of old City Hall, at Wall and Nassau streets. Other potters—many, German immigrants like Crolius—joined him there to take advantage of abundant deposits of natural clay. They established a guild of potters in New York City—the first such organization among manufacturers of stoneware in the colonies.

In 1883 Clarkson Crolius, Jr., claimed that for a hundred years, you could not sail to any part of the world without finding a stoneware mug or jug bearing the stamp *Clarkson Crolius, Manhattan Wells, New York*. Hyperbole aside, what started as a small workshop in the early-eighteenth century flourished in the nineteenth. New York State as a whole, with its abundant sources of clay, plentiful timber for fueling kilns, and well-developed waterways for transporting finished goods to market—became a leader in stoneware production. In fact, potteries in

An 1804 BROADSIDE *advertising the stoneware vessels available from Clarkson Crolius's workshop. Library Collection, Miscellaneous Manuscripts Crolius, Wm F., Crolius notebook, 1827*

Albany, Troy, Utica, Rome, Ithaca, Binghamton, Cortland, Brooklyn, and Poughkeepsie, in addition to New York City, created more stoneware during the nineteenth century than any other state in the union.

Ultimately, the discovery of better ways to seal containers made of glass and tin rendered more unwieldy stoneware storage vessels nearly obsolete. Although passing from everyday use, these items did not disappear entirely from view. Collectors of American folk art identified their simple shapes and charming decoration as worthy of appreciation. Clarkson Crolius's batter pitcher reached the New-York Historical Society in 1937, part of Elie and Viola Nadelman's famous collection of folk art.

The Cartoonist
Who Brought Down Tammany Hall

PRODUCED IN 1871, this stoneware jug was presented to the celebrated New York City cartoonist Thomas Nast (1840-1902) by its makers, Cornwall Kirkpatrick (1814-1890) and his brother Wallace (1828-1896) of the Anna Potteries in Anna, Illinois. Squirming snakes with human faces cover the jug, each representing a different member of New York's corrupt "Tammany Hall" political gang headed up by William Marcy "Boss" Tweed (1823-1878).

STONEWARE JUG *decorated with snakes, each representing a member of William Marcy "Boss" Tweed's gang. Gift of Mrs. Thomas Nast, 1906.6ab*

These infamous politicians and political appointees controlled the governments of New York City and State during the 1860s and early 1870s. The jug parodies the gang's outrageous misappropriation of public funds by depicting its members trying to climb into the money pot. The neck of the jug features the head of Thomas Nast—whose caricatures of Tweed and his ring were instrumental in ousting them from power.

Tweed and his henchmen slithered their way into all municipal undertakings. They defrauded the city of millions of dollars by selling jobs, padding construction bills, and sometimes resorting to outright theft. Best known among the ring's many outrageous scams was the remodeling of the County Court House, which began in 1862. An estimated two-thirds of the total thirteen-million-dollar cost went to padded bills or invoices for nonexistent items. An audit of the city's accounts revealed alarming expenditures; a single carpenter made off with $360,747.61 for one month's work.

Although the court house was just part of the two-hundred-million-dollar fraud that the Tweed Ring perpetrated on the City of New York, its startling excess aroused the suspicions of critics in rival political camps. Thomas Nast waged his campaign against the Tweed Ring from the bulwark of Republicanism, *Harper's Weekly*. Week after week beginning in January of 1870, the cartoonist lashed out at Boss Tweed, dressing him in prison stripes, exaggerating his features, and depicting Democratic Tammany Hall as a rapacious tiger devouring the city. Tweed proceeded to divert the city's advertising budget to muzzle the press. Some eighty-nine papers were placed on the payroll, and Nast himself was offered five-hundred thousand dollars to cease his attacks on Tweed—one hundred times his annual salary at *Harper's Weekly*. Yet Nast persisted and effectively aroused public suspicion against the ring where other powerful

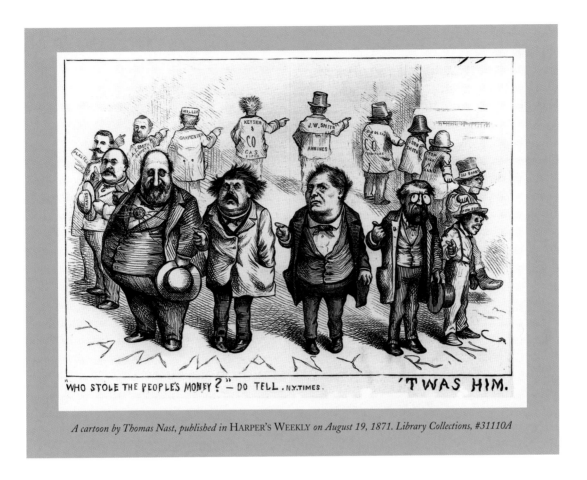

A cartoon by Thomas Nast, published in Harper's Weekly *on August 19, 1871. Library Collections, #31110A*

publications had failed. *Harper's Weekly* reached a wide audience of sympathetic Republicans, but perhaps more importantly, it reached the poor and immigrant population catered to by Tammany Hall itself, which was—as Tweed himself recognized—particularly receptive to visual, rather than verbal, critiques. Nast's cartoons eroded the loyalty of Tweed's primary constituency. The *New York Times* went on to publish irrefutable evidence of widespread graft and corruption in July of 1871, and in 1872 an enraged electorate swept Tweed's gang from power. The Boss was thrown in jail.

The influence of Nast's cartoons did not end there. When Tweed escaped from prison four years later and fled to Spain disguised as a sailor, he was recognized by an avid reader of *Harper's Weekly* and handed over to Spanish officials. Foiled a second time by Thomas Nast, Tweed returned to New York to end his spectacular career behind bars.

Some historians suggest that Tweed was no more dishonest than bosses in scores of other corrupt American cities—only more successful, and perhaps more visible. Tweed became a national symbol of the bloated, big-city boss, and his courthouse, the archetype of the graft-ridden municipal project. This jug, one of many novel pieces that the Kirkpatrick brothers created to record the political events of their day, attests not only to Tweed's notoriety, but also to Nast's popularity as the cartoonist who reversed public apathy toward municipal corruption and helped oust Tweed's gang from power.

Commemorating General Lafayette's Return

NO EVENT IN the history of the early republic caused as much excitement, celebration, and unification as the return of the Marquis de Lafayette (1757-1834) in 1824. The great French statesmen and one of the last surviving heroes of the American Revolution, who had left the comforts of home in 1777 to engage in the War of Independence as a "volunteer of Liberty," was welcomed back to the United States with open arms. Lafayette's August 16 landing at Castle Garden, located at the southern tip of Manhattan, is commemorated in the two large scenes that decorate this mammoth punch bowl. Lafayette's ship, the steamboat *Chancellor Livingston*, is shown surrounded by boats. Pennants and flags fly from every rope and mast. Cannons fire, as a large crowd of admirers (estimated at two-hundred thousand at the actual event) look on from the shore of the Hudson River.

The real-life scene that inspired these images was repeated hundreds of times during the following year. Encouraged by his warm reception in America, Lafayette extended his tour of the original thirteen states to include all twenty-four in the union. Everywhere Lafayette went, the "Nation's Guest" was celebrated, both for his heroics on the American battlefield and as a symbol of the universal cause of freedom. Plagued by growing factionalism and by the mounting debate over how best to extend republican principles and institutions westward, a generation of Americans had begun to fear a backsliding from the country's revolutionary ideals. Lafayette served as a model of faithful commitment to those founding beliefs. His presence created a groundswell of exuberant nationalism throughout the country.

The twenty-two gallon earthenware punch bowl was originally believed to have held the libations served to Lafayette and other guests at the banquet given in the general's honor upon his arrival at Castle Garden. Although the bowl may have held punch, the story of its illustrious past does not hold water. The scene of Lafayette's return to New York is based on an engraving published only after the general's arrival and depicts architectural features of Castle Garden not added until years later. The bowl could not have been made before 1830. Most likely, it was produced in France or England and decorated in the United States as a commemorative souvenir. A pitcher found decorated with the same images suggests that the punch bowl may have originally been part of a larger Castle Garden set.

Many prints and ceramics featuring scenes of Lafayette's triumphant return were produced between 1824 and 1825, as were bottles, flasks, snuff boxes, and other items. Purchased by patriots eager to own reminders of the day Lafayette appeared in their town, these souvenirs and related Lafayette ephemera are now scattered among private collectors, museums, and historical societies throughout the country.

Descendants of the punch bowl's original owner, Christopher Heiser, presented this souvenir to the New-York Historical Society in 1910. What brought the bowl into Heiser's hands may have had as much to do with its depiction of Castle Garden as it did with its veneration of Lafayette. Heiser was the proprietor of the former military fort-turned-entertainment venue, between 1843 and 1852, and may have used the punch bowl—and its alleged associations with the Revolutionary War hero—to promote his establishment as a site for concerts, balls, and other public gatherings.

Massive PUNCH BOWL *commemorating Lafayette's return to America in 1824.*
Gift of Rosalie M. Heiser and John Jay Heiser, 1910.24

Through the Glass Darkly

THE HISTORY OF glass objects can be as cloudy as the pieces are clear. They typically are not marked with the maker's name—as silver items often are—and these particular lead glass pieces bear no inscription. In order to identify and date such objects, curators and historians must piece together clues from their appearance, manufacture, and history of ownership.

Here, experts first compared the form and decoration of this glass to other examples with documented histories. At first glance, the decoration on these pieces—cut in patterns known as strawberry-diamonds and fans—would suggest that they were made in England or Ireland in the early nineteenth century. Strawberry-diamonds were a favorite motif of English glass cutters, and pieces decorated with this overall geometric pattern—called "rich cut" because of the complexity of their design, and the quality of their cutting—commanded high prices.

But although the overall form of these pieces follows English models, their squat bodies and scalloped lips relate them to American forms and suggest that they are products of America, and most likely of New York. Some glass made in imitation of popular English models was produced in the colonies during the eighteenth century, but not until after the War of Independence did the quality of domestic wares begin to rival that of the motherland. Beautiful American-made cut glass was available between 1807 and 1814 (at one-half the price of British wares), but heavy tariffs levied on

Cut-glass COMPOTE WITH COVER *from about 1825. Gift of Lena Cadwalader Evans, 1936.693ab*

English goods after 1824 substantially increased the production of domestic glass in the English style. In light of their shape and decoration, curators believe that these pieces may have been produced in New York between 1823 and 1845. The unusual weight and startling clarity of this glass led early scholars to attribute it to the Brooklyn Flint Glass Works. John Loftus Gilliland, who established the business around 1820, gained an international reputation for the quality of his glass, of which only a few examples survive. The more scholars learn about the Brooklyn Flint Glass Works, however, the less they can say for certain about its wares. On the one hand, Gilliland's advertisements do not mention cut glass before 1840; on the other, the factory was known to supply blanks to independent decorators in New York and Philadelphia, who cut them and then shipped the finished wares as far away as New Orleans. What part, if any, Gilliland's glass works had in the manufacture of these pieces can not be said for certain based on physical evidence alone.

Family records and remembrances offer a few valuable clues to the history of these items. According to Lena Cadwalader Evans (b. 1847), who donated them to the New-York Historical Society in 1936, they were originally owned by one of her great-grand-mothers, Angeline Burr Ketchum (1796-1880) of Connecticut or Abigail Cornell Doty Corse (1776-1854) of New York. Little is known about Ketchum, but the Historical Society's archives document

Lines from the 1842 WILL OF ABIGAIL CORSE, *bequeathing glass and other prized possessions.*
Library, Manuscript Department, Corse Papers

important parts of the Corse family's history. In her will of August 23, 1842, Abigail Corse bequeathed the contents of her home—part of her five-million-dollar estate—to her son Israel Corse, Jr., and her daughter Mary L. Corse Polk. Israel and Mary were to divide their mother's glass equally, along with other items such as carpets, furniture, and china, and Mary was given first choice. The family's written and oral histories do not reveal whether Mary chose this cut glass, but it descended within the Corse family until it reached Evans.

Considered to be the highest quality glass in the society's collection, these items have sparked much debate among scholars but as yet have eluded identification. For now, the history of these pieces remains unclear. New research about the donor's family history, together with evidence from other examples of American glass, may help clarify the mystery of these fragile relics of the past.

Cut-glass DECANTER *from about 1825. Gift of*
Lena Cadwalader Evans, 1936.696ab

A Sumptuous Dish

JOHN W. MACKAY, a poor Irish immigrant, left New York City in 1851 to find his fortune in the California gold mines. He wound up in Nevada, the chief owner of a profitable silver mine, and later became involved in a scheme to make low-grade ore pay by reworking old mines with up-to-date equipment. In 1873, he struck the heart of the Comstock Lode. Virtually overnight, Mackay became the most spectacular mining success in the history of the American West.

A year later, Mackay's wife traveled from the couple's home in Paris, France, to see the "veritable mountain of silver" buried in the depths of the Comstock. In 1867 Mackay had married Marie Louise Hungerford Bryant, a Brooklyn-born woman raised in California and Nevada who, having recently been widowed, was working as a seamstress; by the early 1870s, Bryant had had enough of mining life and left Nevada, first for San Francisco, and then for New York. When East Coast society shunned her, she moved to Paris. The story goes that in the mine, some fifteen-hundred-feet below ground, Marie Mackay asked her husband if she might have enough silver to make some "memorable thing." "Be damned if I won't bring it up for you myself," he replied. "Enough" silver turned out to be more than half a ton. It was used to create one of the most unforgettable dinner services in the history of silver-making.

The silver bullion was shipped directly from the Comstock Lode to Tiffany & Co., reputedly the finest and most fashionable maker of silver tableware in the country. Tiffany's "Dinner and Dessert Service for Twenty-four Persons," designed by Charles Grosjean (d. 1888) exclusively for the Mackays and manufactured between 1877 and 1878, was the largest and most ornate service of its time. Its 1,250 pieces, incorporating designs of flowers and plants from Asia, Persia, and India, employed two hundred men for over two years. Each piece was customized with Marie Louise Hungerford Bryant Mackay's initials, "MLM," and the Hungerford family coat-of-arms, which combined the Scottish thistle and Irish shamrock of her ancestors.

This silver-gilt ice cream dish is decorated with flowers and vines and stands on four feet shaped like elephant trunks. It would have been paired on the Mackay's table with a second ice cream dish, accompanied by twenty-four individual ice cream plates.

A silver-bound book that catalogued the service captures the sumptuous lifestyle this elaborate service supported. Accompanying complete place settings of flatware and serving pieces for every imaginable food were meat dishes with hot water stands, olive dishes, cheese dishes, grape dishes, a punch bowl, a soup tureen, celery vases, gravy tureens, pepper boxes, mustard pots, wine coolers, claret jugs, goblets, a chocolate pot, a syrup jug, crumb trays, a centerpiece, two salon lamps, and two candelabras with two trays holding extinguishers. The list concludes with an example of true Victorian whimsy—two bottle wagons, complete with small, inset wheels that could be sent rolling along the tabletop to deliver drinks between guests at opposite ends of the table.

Before the service was delivered to the Mackays it was exhibited in the American Pavilion at the 1878 Paris Exposition, where it caught the attention of the international press. Although criticized by some for its excess, it was universally recognized as a tour-de-force in silver-making. At the close of the exposition, the service was packed into nine custom-built mahogany chests and carried by thirty-six porters to the Mackay's home just off the Champs-Elysées, where it was used at a series of spectacular banquets. The seamstress once snubbed by New York circles had become a leader of European society. A brilliant hostess, Mrs. Mackay entertained European royalty on her Tiffany service and grew famous for her parties, landmarks in an era of elaborate entertainments.

"The millionaire who ordered it, the enterprising firm which undertook the commission, the artist who settled the composition and the design, the craftsmen who wrought their work into actual silver, were the victim of one and the same idea. The service is a monument of the wealth of the owner. To put as much silver into it as possible, to put as much work on the silver as possible, to impress the beholder at the same time with the enormous costliness of the service and the skill of its makers—is apparently the object, and is beyond question the effect, of this large accumulation of coin and cunning."

—*New York Daily Tribune*, 1878

Tiffany & Co. ICE CREAM DISH, *part of a large service made for John and Marie Mackay with silver from the Comstock Lode. Gift of John Mackay, 1980.14*

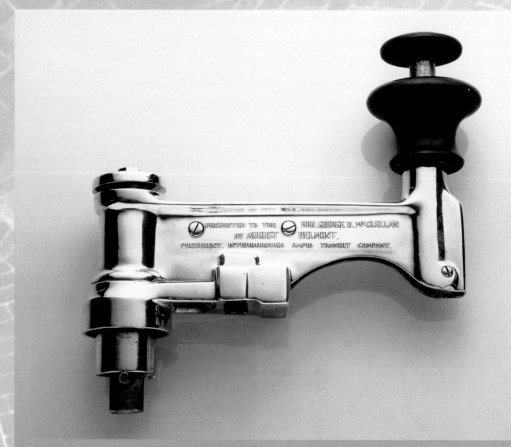

Silver CONTROLLER HANDLE *by Tiffany & Co., used on the maiden voyage of New York City's first subway.*
Gift of George B. McClellan, 1922.103

Rapid Transit Made Real

AT 2:35 P.M. ON OCTOBER 27, 1904, New York City Mayor George B. McClellan (1865-1940) grabbed this silver handle and commandeered the first subway train on its maiden voyage from City Hall to 145th Street. Intoxicated by the speed, McClellan blew through the scheduled station stop at 42nd Street and continued uptown, only yielding the controls to the company's conductor at 103rd Street. The trip to 145th Street took precisely twenty-six minutes. New York's long-standing dream of rapid transit had come true.

At street level, transit was anything but rapid. Manhattan's thoroughfares were choked with slow-moving traffic, as a constant stream of horse-drawn carts and carriages moved along two-way streets unregulated by traffic lights.

The elevated train, trolley cars, and ferries offered some relief, but by 1860 New Yorkers had already recognized the need for a rapid transit system. Proposals for an underground system were made in the early 1890s, but no private companies were willing to risk the investment. The plan for a city-funded underground rapid transit system was finally approved in 1894.

A carnival atmosphere prevailed as New Yorkers celebrated the opening of the subway. Large crowds gathered at the entrances to each station, and over one-hundred and sixty-five thousand people went underground to experience the subway for the first time. As much as New Yorkers had talked about the subway, they were unprepared for the new experiences it offered. Waiting crowds were shocked by the unusual sight of riders emerging from the stations—first heads, then shoulders, then finally bodies, seemingly sprouting from the earth. The sensation of traveling underground was even more startling. Passengers commented on the "queer and unfamiliar air" that filled the stations and the sight of racing trains suddenly emerging from the total darkness of the tunnels into the light of the white-tiled stations.

The subway not only provided a new experience of physical space and speed; it collapsed the sense of distance that divided New York's heterogeneous communities. Linking New York with its surrounding areas had been part of the overall plan of the rapid transit system from the start. Following the consolidation of the five boroughs into an administrative whole in 1898, that plan became a necessity. At a ceremony held at City Hall on the day the subway opened, McClellan remarked, "Without rapid transit, Greater New York would be little more than a geographical expression." When the first phase of the new system opened in 1908, with 714 miles of track covering a distance of 244 miles, Greater New York became a geographical reality. Although the Brooklyn Bridge remains the icon of modern urbanization and unification most celebrated by artists and poets, the less visible underground rapid transit system effectively united Manhattan, Brooklyn, the Bronx, and Queens, helping to re-conceptualize the city into what McClellan termed, "the mightiest metropolis the world has ever seen."

The opening of the City Hall subway station, *1903. Print Room, Negative File, #29079A*

A Sight for Sore Eyes

LOUIS COMFORT TIFFANY (1848-1933), of New York's prominent jewelry retailing family Tiffany & Co., introduced his now-famous Tiffany lamps around 1899. Long valued as amazing works of art in their own right, they were actually created as a by-product of another Tiffany item developed earlier—his stained-glass windows. The lamp shades, which are made by setting small pieces of colored glass into a lead frame, solved a problem for Tiffany: what to do with all the unusable glass left over from making his stained-glass windows.

Tiffany began his artistic career as a landscape painter, and his love of nature informed all of his artistic production. His stained-glass windows—in essence, landscapes painted with glass—recorded nature in intricate detail. During his travels in Spain, Morocco, and North Africa, Tiffany became fascinated with the effects of light passing through glass and reflecting off surfaces like bronze and ceramic tile. In attempting to duplicate the sumptuous effects of light he discovered the limitations of commercially made glass available in the United States. He experimented for years with the goal of developing glass in brilliant colors, free of the paints and pigments that interfered with the full transmission of light. The Tiffany Glass Company, founded in 1885, patented four types of glass over the course of two decades. Its factory in Corona, Queens, produced glass in a seemingly limitless range of colors and textures for use in his windows.

In 1900, the artist expanded his operations, founding Tiffany Studios, and began creating lamps and other decorative objects with glass.

The lamps designed by Tiffany Studios render fruits and flowers in vivid color. Depicted at different stages of bloom, hydrangeas, hollyhocks, wisteria, and apple blossoms unfold on the shades, at times breaking the border and spilling over the sides. Tiffany also depicted living creatures, such as bats and insects. In the "drophead dragonfly" design, the heads of the dragonflies burst the frame, their bodies extending upward to about the middle of the shade. The brilliant orange of their wings, extensively mottled with mauve and gray, contrasts with the dark blue and green glass used to render the water. Blue jewel eyes and the undulating, knobby glass used in the bodies of the insects give them a visceral quality. The extensive mixing of half-round and fibrillated glass in

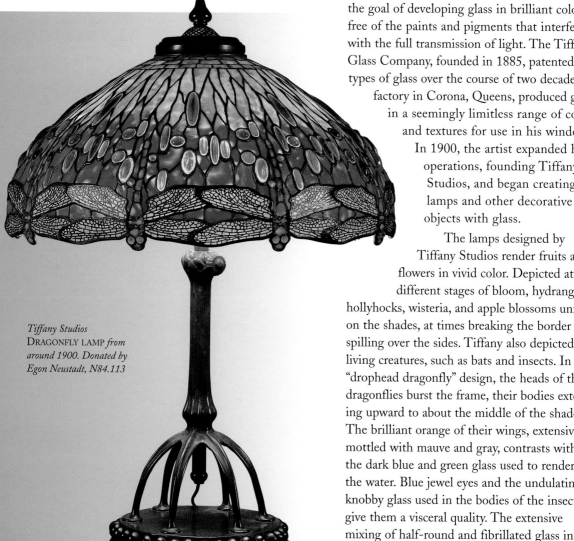

Tiffany Studios DRAGONFLY LAMP *from around 1900. Donated by Egon Neustadt, N84.113*

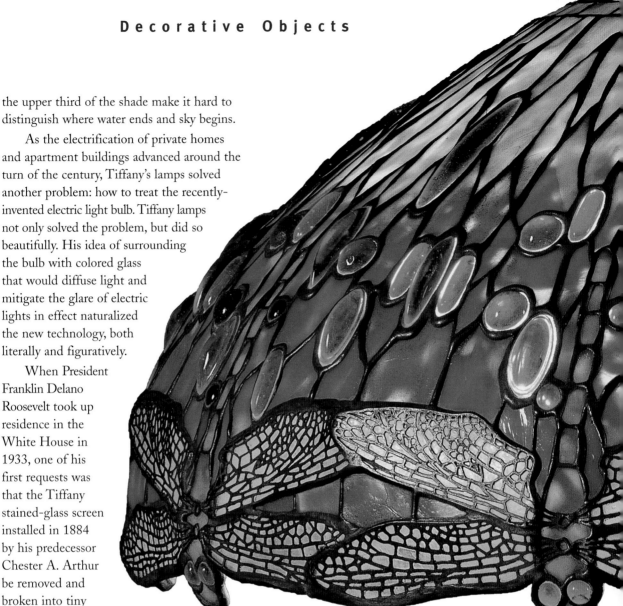

the upper third of the shade make it hard to distinguish where water ends and sky begins.

As the electrification of private homes and apartment buildings advanced around the turn of the century, Tiffany's lamps solved another problem: how to treat the recently-invented electric light bulb. Tiffany lamps not only solved the problem, but did so beautifully. His idea of surrounding the bulb with colored glass that would diffuse light and mitigate the glare of electric lights in effect naturalized the new technology, both literally and figuratively.

When President Franklin Delano Roosevelt took up residence in the White House in 1933, one of his first requests was that the Tiffany stained-glass screen installed in 1884 by his predecessor Chester A. Arthur be removed and broken into tiny pieces. Tiffany Studios had ceased production around 1928 and its products had fallen out of fashion. Many of the firm's decorative objects were relegated to the attic or, alternately, the junk heap.

In 1935, Dr. Egon Neustadt and his wife Hildegard began collecting lamps, windows, and other items produced by Tiffany Studios. Over the next fifty years, these pioneer collectors of Tiffany lamps amassed an astounding collection, the most comprehensive of its kind. In 1984, Neustadt donated one-hundred and thirty-two lamps and five landscape panels to the New-York Historical Society. The variety of their

shapes, sizes, and colors, reveals the full range of Tiffany's artistic production. Housed in the Luce Center alongside other decorative objects collected by the Historical Society, they bear witness to the genius of one of New York State's most unique artistic productions.

Tools for Home and Trade

The New-York Historical Society's collection of tools used in the home, on the farm, or in workshops and offices, contributes to an understanding of the pace and habits of everyday life in New York over time. Items as diverse as a butter churn and a mimeograph provide insight on the new types of work—as well as a new rhythm of work—that emerged in the late-nineteenth and early-twentieth centuries. From a set of iron fireplace tongs to Edison's Universal Stock Ticker, objects in this category span the time period from the Dutch Colonial era to the early-twentieth century.

Some objects were collected for their historical associations or as folk art, but many—acquired between the 1920s and the 1950s—were added to the collection simply to preserve ways of life that were perceived as disappearing in the New York City region, as the landscape and technologies for home and work environments changed.

Included in the collection are a wide variety of items related to food preparation, such as iron pots and pans for the open fireplace, long-handled toasters, copper tea-kettles, cake-molds, butter churns, corn huskers, meat grinders, sausage stuffers, mortars and pestles, and chopping knives. Items related to household maintenance or trade-work done out of the home—such as clothes wringers, spinning and weaving implements, and sewing utensils— are also included, as are neck-yokes used for carrying buckets, a wooden rack for dipping candles, a washtub hollowed out of a tree trunk, and a rope-making machine. Nineteenth-century plows, axes, hog yokes, cow bells, and a bear trap provide clues to an agrarian past, when parts of New York City were farmland and forest.

Tools of various trades and professions, such as a cobbler's bench (complete with shoe forms), ice tongs, eel traps, opticians' tools, typewriters, photographic equipment, a shock therapy machine from the 1850s, and a pill rolling machine, create vivid pictures of the diverse work environments that existed in the past. Artists' tools and equipment, like the desk used by miniature painter John Ramage, or the contents of Asher B. Durand's studio at the time of his death, remind us of the technical skills involved in being an artist.

Many of the objects in this category were originally part of the George W. Nash Collection of Household Artifacts, assembled in Ulster County, New York. Nash had an antiquarian interest in domestic items that reflected New York's Dutch colonial days. His collection was given to the society in 1920 by one of its former presidents, Samuel V. Hoffman. The Historical Society still collects tools for home and trade, both for their antiquarian interest and for the glimpse of technological progress and social change that they provide.

Making a Fine Impression

Viola and Elie Nadelman purchased this double-sided cake board in the early twentieth century and added it to their extensive collection of American and European folk art. A century earlier, utensils like this one—along with butter molds, cookie cutters, and pudding molds—had been used to create folk art of an edible kind.

Made from mahogany, walnut, pear, cherry, linden, or beech, cake boards were produced by cabinetmakers, carpenters, and wood carvers. They were used to imprint low-relief designs onto stiff doughs like gingerbread, marzipan, and springerle (used because they tended to rise only slightly during baking). Thinly rolled dough was pressed into the mold and peeled away to leave a crisp impression, and then allowed to air-dry before baking. After baking, the cakes (today's cookies) were decorated with frosting or a sprinkling of colored sugar. Although typically baked in time for Christmas, New Year's, or Easter celebrations, the finished cakes would keep for months. The often-repeated saying goes that, after a while, the cakes became so hard that it was just as easy to eat the cake board as it was to eat the cake.

This particular example may have been made by John Conger (1803-1869), a New York City artisan who practiced his craft during the second quarter of the nineteenth century. Favorites among folk art collectors, Conger's cake boards are easily identified by their oval or elliptical borders and are valued for their precise carving, which would have produced highly legible designs on cakes. Conger had an inside line on making cake boards: in addition to being a master carver, he was also a baker.

Conger developed a repertoire of distinctive patterns to use in combination on his cake boards. These patterns, or stock motifs, included cornucopias, garlands, flower baskets, eagles, roses, thistles, Revolutionary War soldiers, Native Americans, militia men on horseback, ladies and gentlemen dressed in rustic garb, and other romantic images, many of which were considered old-fashioned even in the mid-nineteenth century.

Another favorite motif of Conger's was the fire truck. This cake board features two images of fire engines, both pulled by three firemen: one is labeled "Manhattan" and "8," and the other, "Superior" and "17." The styles of the firefighters' hats and coats suggest that this piece was designed between 1825 and 1835. The New-York Historical Society purchased the mold, along with hundreds of other pieces of folk art, from Elie Nadelman in 1937.

Two other cake boards attributed to Conger are housed in the society's collection. One features the figures of "Britannia," "Greece," and "America" beneath an eagle with outstretched wings. The other illustrates General Lafayette on horseback. Closely tied to the popular historical events of their day, these molds were most likely used by commercial bakers located along the Bowery in the first half of the nineteenth century. These cakes were probably made in quantity and sold at parades and other public events, such as those celebrating Lafayette's return to the United States in 1824. Cakes featuring fire engines were perhaps produced commercially as well, and may have been sold at the numerous parades, sporting events, and competitions held between rival volunteer fire companies throughout the second quarter of the nineteenth century.

DOUBLE-SIDED CAKE BOARD, *probably carved by John Conger between 1825 and 1835. Purchased from Elie Nadelman, 1937.1562*

When Doctors Made House-calls

THESE LEATHER SADDLEBAGS hung alongside the hindquarters of Dr. Myron Orton's horse. Orton (1784-1873) began working as a country doctor in 1811 in Niagara County. He joined the local militia during the War of 1812, serving as a physician to the troops, and resumed his practice after the war. He most likely covered a wide area on horseback, making house-calls and attending to the myriad medical needs of settlers in upstate New York, until ending his career around 1850.

When the saddlebags were given to the New-York Historical Society in 1954, their divided compartment contained four glass vials, each containing medicine prescribed by Dr. Orton to his patients. Some of these drugs were no doubt used in the doctor's attempt to restore the equilibrium of their "humors." According to the theory of disease then current, illness was caused by an imbalance of four substances—blood, phlegm, choler, and black bile—which could be restored to equilibrium by means of purging, sweating, blistering, and above all bloodletting. One thing Dr. Orton's bag probably did not contain were anesthetics, used to deaden pain. Anesthetics were first introduced in a surgical procedure in 1842; child birthing, tooth extraction, and other procedures performed by Orton would have been performed without its benefits.

Medical practice as we know it today differed in many other ways from that of the early nineteenth century. The elaborate system of specialized knowledge combined with technical procedure had not yet been developed in this country, and a physician's private practice took on a character unique to his particular interests and skills. Doctors began practicing at an early age, after completing only two years of study, often without a clinical component. In the years following the American Revolution, medical societies were established and licensing authority was extended to them by state legislatures, but no standards of education or practical instruction were set. What's more, a license was not required to practice medicine. Practiced in conjunction with Dr. Orton's brand of medicine were the equally legitimate medicines of the domestic household and of the lay healer.

PHYSICIAN'S SADDLEBAGS AND MEDICINES, *used by Dr. Myron Orton in the first half of the nineteenth century. Gift of Mrs. E. L. Woolf, 1954.11*

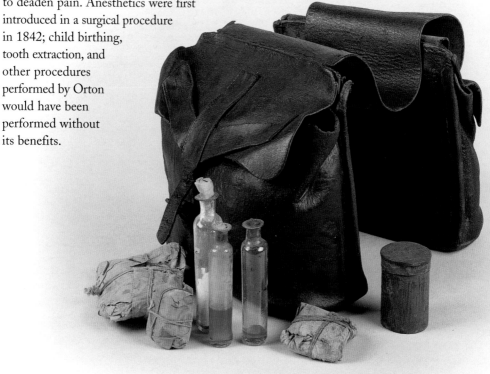

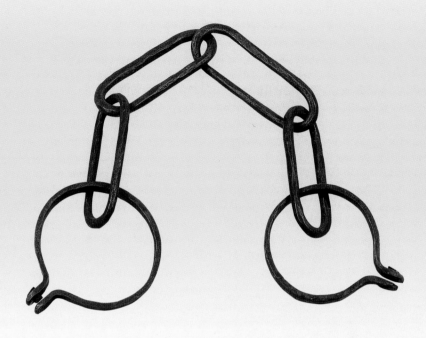

SHACKLES, *cut from the ankles of a former slave in the spring of 1866. Gift of Mrs. Carroll Beckwith, 1921.20*

Breaking the Bonds of Slavery

WHEN THESE STEEL shackles were presented to the New-York Historical Society, they were accompanied by a card that related their history. Hand-written in April of 1880 by William W. Badger, who served as provost marshal of Sumpter County, Georgia, at the end of the Civil War, that history reads as follows:

> The shackles were cut by me with a cold chisel from the ankles of Mary Horn, a good looking quadroon girl, about seventeen years of age, in Americus, in Sumpter County, Georgia, in the spring of 1866, more than a year after the slaves were freed; I being then Lieut. Colonel of the 176th Regiment New York Volunteers, the last New York Regiment to return from that state.
>
> Mary Horn had been a slave of Judge Horn, a prominent Confederate of this county, who riveted these irons on her with his own hands so that she could never remove them. His object was to prevent her from going to her lover, George, on the next plantation; George complained to me, and held the girl over an anvil while I cut the rivets. I then married them and told him to

protect her by force if necessary, which he did, by killing Judge Horn in a riot six months later.

The story associated with these slave shackles is not uncommon: during the early period of Reconstruction, resistance to anti-slavery legislation delayed the freeing of untold numbers of slaves. The continued presence of the 176th Regiment, New York Volunteers in Georgia attests to the fact that the transition from slavery to emancipation was a difficult one. What is more uncommon is the survival of the artifacts themselves; shackles, slave tags, and other items related to the "peculiar institution" of slavery are extremely rare, and the existence of a documented history of their use is almost unique.

The Historical Society received the shackles as a gift from Mrs. Carroll Beckwith in 1921. They augmented a collection of over twenty-one thousand pamphlets, sixty-five hundred manuscripts, and twelve-hundred photographs formed in 1914 through a gift of Daniel Parish, Jr.,—one of the earliest collections of material relating to African-American life, the Civil War, and Reconstruction in this country.

Sign that hung outside the office of JOHN B.
SNOOK & SONS, *designer of A. T. Stewart's
famous New York emporium. Gift of Thomas E.
Snook, Jr., 1953.197*

THIS SIGN HUNG outside the office of architects
J. B. Snook & Sons. Jonathan Butler Snook
(1815-1901), who began practicing in New York
in 1837, was fond of ornamenting his multi-
story warehouses with vigorous Corinthian
capitals and bulbous Tuscan columns. But the
resemblance of his work to ancient Greek and
Roman architecture ended there: from the mid-
1850s onward, Snook created his ornaments out
of cast iron. Mass-produced in foundries and
shipped to construction sites, these pieces were
quickly assembled into commercial structures—
filled with air and light—that came to dominate
the city south of Houston Street. Having established a niche, Snook maintained a successful
and prolific practice until the end of the century.

The building that established Snook's
professional career was executed in collaboration
with Joseph Trench (1815-1879), the architect
with whom he had apprenticed. Snook was a
junior partner in Trench's firm when, in 1845,
Irish-born merchant Alexander T. Stewart
commissioned his Dry Goods Store on Broadway
and Chambers Street. In the most dramatic and
innovative move of his career, Stewart defied
conventional wisdom about successful merchan-
dising and created a grand retail emporium
that would sell ready-made goods organized
by department. From the time of its opening
in 1846, the building—and its merchandise—
created a sensation. The gleaming marble façade
and large plate-glass windows were like nothing
Stewart's customers had ever seen before. Inside,
curly maple and mahogany counters and shelves
stocked a staggering variety of goods—from
four-thousand-dollar shawls to packets of pins—
displayed throughout several floors.

The space was designed to entice the
shopper. A rotunda spanned the entire width
of the building, its domed skylight admitting
abundant sunshine. A flight of stairs with
gleaming balustrades coaxed buyers past items
on the main selling floor and into the upper
stories, where each room of goods opened onto
a gallery overlooking the rotunda. As contem-
poraries noted, this gallery provided a place "for
the ladies to promenade upon"—or in today's
parlance, a place for shoppers to see and be
seen. A. T. Stewart's Dry Goods Store quickly
became New York's most fashionable emporium,
as much for the spectacle as for the luxury
merchandise it sold. The first department store
in the world and an innovative building type,
the "Marble Palace" laid the foundation for
Stewart's subsequent success as a retailer, and
Snook's success as an architect as well.

Trench departed for the West Coast shortly after A. T. Stewart's store was completed, and Snook continued the practice on his own. He moved to Brooklyn in 1860 and was gradually joined in business by his three sons and one son-in-law. Together, father and sons built some of the most impressive buildings in New York, including several houses for the Vanderbilts and the original Grand Central Depot. When John

B. Snook died in 1901, the firm was carried on by his sons and grandsons. In 1953, Thomas Snook, Jr., presented the New-York Historical Society with two hundred rolls of the firm's drawings, a collection of company ledgers and account books, and the sign that had hung outside his grandfather's office.

Drawing of the Reade Street façade of the expanded A. T. STEWART DRY GOODS STORE *from 1859. Print Room, John B. Snook Architectural Record Collection, #53487*

Private Life and Public Service

Archeological artifacts; badges, medals, and ribbons; firefighting equipment; jewelry; military items; personal accessories; public and civic artifacts; souvenirs; textiles and needlework; toys and dolls: from groups of objects as diverse as these come the stories discussed in this chapter. Each of these categories has its own significant donors and discrete collecting history, which often span the entire life of the New-York Historical Society. Some categories, such as textiles, encompass a single medium, but most consist of objects made of a variety of media, grouped according to use.

Those uses, as the title of this chapter suggests, can be understood according to the rubric of "Private Life and Public Service." Personal items, such as the wedding rings and mourning brooches in the jewelry collection, which passed between husband and wife, mother and daughter, over generations before coming to the society, relate to private life. Grapeshot, insignia, and weaponry—all involved with service in the military—relate to public service. Some objects, however, fall into both categories, such as a mechanical bank, designed in the form of a bloated Tammany Hall politician; or a wig curler, excavated from the site of a Revolutionary War camp, thought to have been used to dress the hair of a British Army officer or his wife.

What most of these objects speak to is a kind of identity—be it a public one or private one, or a combination of the two. These objects and their histories cast light on what it meant to be a citizen, a patriot, an officer, a bride, a slave, a child, a collector, a leader, a supporter, a detractor, a role model, a New Yorker. The most diverse group of objects considered in this book, they are also some of the most articulate about the past.

Altering Convention

CORNELIA DE PEYSTER (b. 1690) donned this vibrant yellow-and-cream silk brocade dress on October 12, 1712, at her marriage to Oliver Stephen Teller (b. 1685). The dress probably looks somewhat different today than it did on that fall day.

Made of the most luxurious and costly material a bride's family could afford, wedding dresses worn in the colonial period in New York were often considered too precious to be put away and never worn again. After the wedding ceremony, they were often integrated into a lady's wardrobe and worn at other formal occasions. During de Peyster's marriage to Teller, this dress was probably cut in a loose-fitting style called a mantua, which was popular throughout the seventeenth and eighteenth centuries. It was most likely re-styled in about 1750 into a *robe á l'anglaise*, and worn again by the bride or her descendants to balls and other social occasions.

In a Dutch colonial family such as the Tellers', clothing that survived frequent use and cleaning would be preserved and passed down to subsequent generations along with other textiles; after silver, textiles constituted a household's most valued possessions. An important part of a woman's dowry, they were often specifically mentioned in wills and were passed down to ensure the wealth of a loved one.

This dress was passed down to de Peyster and Teller's descendants for more than two hundred years. The presence of different sets of colored threads and sizes of stitches indicates that the dress was substantially altered a second time—probably around the turn of the twentieth century. The waistline was re-sewn and the pleated skirt reworked. Nineteenth-century needlepoint lace ruffles were added, the sleeve cuffs were re-styled, and a silk and chiffon modesty panel was attached to the top of the stomacher's square neckline. Alice Crary, a descendant of Cornelia de Peyster, wore this re-styled version of the dress at her marriage to Arthur T. Sutcliffe on April 30, 1908.

What motivated Crary to buck the convention popularized by Queen Victoria of wearing an all-white bridal ensemble has been left unrecorded; the family history and historical significance of the dress—rather than its intrinsic monetary value—seem likely motivations. With the rise of an affluent middle class in the twentieth century, the habit of re-using one's wedding gown for formal occasions has all but disappeared. The wedding dress has become a sentimental treasure, cherished even more highly perhaps for the extravagance of its one-time use.

Mrs. Sutcliffe donated her wedding dress to the New-York Historical Society in 1949.

Today, it is looked upon as an early and important example of colonial costume, related to one of New York's most prominent Dutch families. But it is also seen as valuable evidence of the social patterns and conventions of dress that dictated the use and re-use of such items over time.

Silk brocade WEDDING DRESS *worn in 1712 by Cornelia de Peyster. Gift of Mrs. Arthur T. Sutcliffe, 1949.115a*

Sentimental Charms

WHEN CORNELIA DICKENSON (1744-1816) married Hendrick Remsen, Jr. (1736-1792), on December 28, 1761, she received this silver-gilt chatelaine as a wedding present. This combination watch fob and charm clip, chased in the latest design, was probably made in London and imported to New York, where the Remsens lived. Worn suspended from a waistband or girdle so that it hung by her side, this piece held the personal and sentimental objects she would collect throughout the next thirty years.

Chatelaines were traditionally given to the bride by her new father-in-law. Hendrick Remsen, Sr., the head of a prominent merchant family, would have had easy access to such a fine piece of jewelry—as well as the resources to buy it. Remsen, Jr., followed in his father's footsteps and established his own shop in Hanover Square, which sold a wide variety of imported goods. When women began adding charms to their watch chains in 1790, they may have visited his shop in search of popular trinkets, such as gold or agate seals, heart-shaped lockets, keys, and hair encased in crystal. Useful items were added to the chains as well, including pencils, small mirrors, patch boxes, scent bottles and pomanders containing sweet-smelling powder or paste, pincushions, thimbles, and even scissors. Four charms were added to Cornelia Remsen's chatelaine: a bloodstone container with a hinged lid, a padlock-shaped charm, a coral trumpet, and an oculus.

The most revealing item on this chatelaine is an oval miniature, less than two inches across. The tiny painting on ivory features the Remsens' son Johaunes Henry (1771-1798), the fifth of their nine children to live to maturity. Based on his appearance and style of dress, Johaunes, or John, is about twenty in the painting. In 1793, the young man opened his own store at Albany Pier (now Coenties Slip) and in May of 1798 he married. Four months later, he died of yellow fever. The most feared epidemic of the period, yellow fever was carried to American shores by mosquitoes, chiefly aboard ships from South America and the West Indies. It claimed its most victims that year. Unlike the other more whimsical charms, the miniature, inscribed "John Henry Remsen/B 2 Aug 1771/D 15 Sept 1798," probably served as a mother's bittersweet reminder of a lost child.

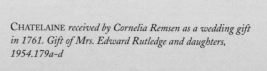

CHATELAINE *received by Cornelia Remsen as a wedding gift in 1761. Gift of Mrs. Edward Rutledge and daughters, 1954.179a-d*

A Fine Leg to Stand On

IN MAY OF 1780, while trying to control a pair of runaway horses in Philadelphia, Gouverneur Morris (1752-1816) was thrown down into the wheels of his own carriage. Morris was bedridden for three months with a badly mangled leg, and when infection set in, amputation was presented as the only option to save his life. The leg was taken off below the knee, and for the next thirty-six years Morris wore this sturdy but primitive wooden limb and others like it. Almost forty inches long and made of turned and carved oak, the prosthesis has a U-shaped knee-rest, lined with green leather. Morris secured the leg to his thigh with a set of ties, threaded through a series of metal slots.

The Revolutionary statesman and orator from New York took his loss with great courage—and a dose of good humor. A friend, who had heard that Morris had had the accident while attempting to escape a jealous husband, once tried to assure him that the incident was a blessing in disguise, since it put certain "temptations" out of his reach. "My dear sir," Morris replied, "you reason so convincingly and you show me so clearly the advantage of being without legs, that I feel almost tempted to get rid of the other one." Strong and vigorous, standing six feet, four-inches tall, Morris nevertheless continued to charm the ladies: at the age of sixty-one, he married Anne Carey Randolph of Virginia.

The loss of his leg did not prevent Morris from continuing an already distinguished career of public service. From 1781 to 1785, he was assistant to Robert Morris (no relation), superintendent of finance for the young republic. He was elected to the Pennsylvania delegation to the Constitutional Convention of 1787, where he used his incomparable writing skills to help shape the Constitution into its final literary form. The leading American in Paris during the French Revolution, Morris served as George Washington's minister to France from 1792 until 1794. He continued to ride in carriages during his service in France, even though the vehicles had been banned as "aristocratic." Confronted by angry cries of "An aristocrat!" as he rode through the streets of Paris one day, Morris is said to have quietly opened the door of his carriage and thrust out his wooden leg, claiming (less than honestly), "Yes, truly, who lost his leg in the cause of American liberty." The mob met this comment with a round of applause.

Morris returned to the New York in 1799, where he served briefly in the U.S. Senate, advocated on behalf of the Erie Canal, and acted as first vice-president, and later president of the New-York Historical Society. His artificial limb joined the society's collection in 1954, the gift of Morris's great-granddaughter.

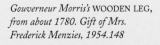

Gouverneur Morris's WOODEN LEG, *from about 1780. Gift of Mrs. Frederick Menzies, 1954.148*

Caps Off to the Grenadiers

THIS CAP WAS purchased by the New-York Historical Society at an antiques shop in New London, Connecticut. Hand-made of coarse wool dyed bright red and blue, this tall, triangular cap is beautifully embroidered in white and yellow yarn. On its front panel, three stanchions entwined with branches and the inscription "AUT VINCE AUT MORI" (meaning "Conquer or Die") surround an eight-pointed star. On the back, a grenade embroidered at its center surrounded by a crossed sword and musket indicate its original use, as the hat of a grenadier in an independent militia company in Connecticut.

Grenadier companies were formed outside of common militias. Financed independently and taking their orders directly from the governor of a colony, they filled their ranks with men of elite standing and affluent backgrounds. Grenadiers were among the tallest and strongest of foot soldiers and were known for their bravery; as a consequence, they were often deployed first during attacks. They were also given the dubious honor of throwing grenades, an extremely risky business. A primitive version of today's weapons, grenades were simply metal spheres packed with gunpowder and ignited with matches.

When the Historical Society purchased this cap in 1890, the shopkeeper claimed that it had been worn by a grenadier during the Revolutionary War, at the Battle of Fort Griswold in nearby Groton. The shopkeeper's assertion probably added to the appeal of the item, in that artifacts dating from that epic period in America's history have consistently been held in the highest esteem. But the claim is debatable. Cloth caps were abolished in the British regular service in 1768 and were replaced by caps made of bearskin; thus, this cap would not have passed muster in 1781, the year of the battle. The cap was more than likely worn before the Revolution, during the French and Indian War, by a grenadier serving in a company raised by the provincial government of Connecticut.

GRENADIER'S CAP, *dating from about 1740 to 1770. Purchased by the Society, 1890.3*

Military scholars have also questioned whether caps such as this one ever saw battle at all. Although some claim that the caps, worn close to the head, allowed grenadiers easy access to muskets carried across their backs, others maintain that the decorative caps were put away when a company was called into service and taken out only on ceremonial occasions.

A Public Display of Affiliation

WHAT DID THEODORE ROOSEVELT, John Jacob Astor, Fiorello H. La Guardia, Al Jolson, and Harry Houdini have in common? All were members of the secret male fraternal organization commonly known as the Freemasons.

Started by English stonemasons in the seventeenth century, the brotherhood reached America in 1730 and claimed for its membership many important figures in colonial society. In 1787 Grand Master Robert R. Livingston (1746-1813), member of the second Continental Congress and a drafter of the Declaration of Independence, led the New York lodges in breaking free from the English organization. His apron and sash, along with the Masonic regalia of many other prominent New Yorkers, are now housed in the Luce Center.

Freemasons advanced a set of moral principles. The simple tools of the stonemason—the square, compass, trowel, and plumb—were used as symbols in teaching these principles, during carefully prescribed ceremonies and rituals. The Freemason's apron was perhaps the single most important piece of regalia worn at these ceremonies. Modeled after medieval stonemasons' protective garb, they were originally made out of plain white lambskin. Over time, Freemasons reduced the size of these emblems of purity and began fashioning them from white cloth.

During the late eighteenth century, when Livingston's regalia was made, Freemasons began to embellish their aprons with the symbols of the mason's craft. In America, aprons were often flamboyantly decorated with silk and metallic threads, either by a family member or by a professional embroiderer. Livingston had his white silk apron lined in light blue and added a matching ruffle to its edges, blue representing the canopy of heaven. The compass and square in the center of the apron are the symbols of reason and faith. The compass is also a symbolic reminder to proscribe or keep passions in check. The single eye represents the all-seeing Supreme Being. The significance of the cord and tasseled rope has yet to be deciphered.

More generic symbols of social virtue such as the American flag may have been included on Livingston's apron in light of the fact that he, like other patriots, frequently appeared at public events wearing Masonic regalia. Such public displays of one's affiliation with the brotherhood reached their peak during the Marquis de Lafayette's 1824 tour of the United States.

Soon after, the reputation of the Freemasons was tarnished by scandal, when a member who had threatened to reveal the secrets of the order was found murdered. Suspicions arose that the Masons were part of a mysterious sect that considered itself above the law. Although Freemasons continued to occupy positions of power within New York society, they did so somewhat less conspicuously until well into the twentieth century, and perhaps still do today.

Grand Master Robert R. Livingston's MASONIC APRON. *Gift of Goodhue Livingston, Jr., 1951.523ab*

Washington Slept Here, Uncomfortably

OF THE MANY objects housed at the New-York Historical Society that were used by George Washington—the Beekman family coach in which he rode through town, the chair he used at his inauguration, the forty-six letters written in his own hand that are part of his official war correspondence—this camp bed is perhaps the most personal. It provides an unmatched glimpse of this extraordinary general's ordinary life during the Revolutionary War.

General Washington is said to have slept in this bed while at Valley Forge. Over six feet long, it has a canvas top supported on X-shaped wooden legs. Organized in three folding sections, the bed could be folded up, placed on the baggage wagon, and transported from campsite to campsite. The bed was originally fitted with a wooden frame supported by iron mounts; three sides of the frame still remain. These boards most likely held mattress padding in place, to make a more comfortable bed for the general.

Mattress padding would have insured only modest comfort, however. For the pitifully equipped Continental Army, camp life— especially in winter—was often miserable. At Valley Forge, officers and soldiers endured the worst winter of the war. When the troops arrived at the Pennsylvania encampment in December of 1777, they pitched what tents they had on frozen earth. Most of the men slept with only a thin layer of straw between them and the ground, covering themselves with blankets that they carried from camp to camp in their knapsacks. Their tents were no match for such harsh conditions and orders went out shortly after the soldiers arrived to fell trees, split out boards, and begin building huts. Working a half-leg deep in snow, often without shoes or stockings, the soldiers constructed a crude log-house city. The legend goes that their commander-in-chief exchanged his own leaky tent—and this camp bed—for the shelter of a nearby home only after all of his men had moved out of their tents and under solid roofs of their own.

At the close of the Revolutionary War, General Washington presented this bed to his recording secretary Richard Varick (1753-1831), whom he had appointed to arrange and copy his voluminous official correspondence. Colonel Varick entrusted it to his wife's niece, Mrs. John L. Lefferts, and she in turn gave it to her great-nephew, Ernest Livingston McCrackan. McCrackan presented the camp bed to Historical Society in January of 1871, along with a letter from his great-aunt, Mrs. Francis A. Livingston, telling of her family's ownership.

CAMP BED *used by General George Washington at Valley Forge. Gift of Ernest Livingston McCrackan,* 1871.8

Martha Washington Sneezed Here

KERCHIEF *from the Revolutionary period, possibly commissioned by Martha Washington.*
Gift of Mrs. J. Insley Blair, 1952.63

IN JUNE OF 1775, Martha Washington (1731-1802) and her husband traveled to Philadelphia, where they visited with Mrs. John Hancock and other friends. During their stay, they heard about a calico printing establishment run by Captain John Hewson. Curious about an industry that had only recently been introduced to the colonies, the Washingtons decided to see Hewson's factory for themselves. Martha Washington was so impressed that she commissioned a handkerchief printed with "His Excellency represented in full military dress on horseback, with a truncheon in his left hand."

Even though the figure of George Washington pictured on this kerchief, holding a drawn sword in his right hand, differs somewhat in its details from Martha Washington's description, it has long been associated with the story of Martha Washington and Captain Hewson. The thirty-inch square of cotton was printed in black and reddish-brown ink. Stock elements such as militia flags, cannons, ramrods, and powder kegs, are surrounded with a floral border. Circling the kerchief's central medallion is the inscription, "George Washington, Esq. Foundator and Protector of America's Liberty and Independency." Within the medallion, the printer placed the equestrian figure of Washington. The general's

image is modeled after a portrait by Alexander Campbell, reproduced as a mezzotint in 1775 by the London printmaker C. Shepard. Although Washington never sat for the Campbell portrait, he was familiar with it; in a letter to Joseph Reed dated January 31, 1776, the statesman joked, "Mr. Campbell has made a very formidable figure of the Commander-in-Chief, giving him a sufficient portion of terror in his countenance." In contrast to the original, Washington presents a commanding image in the version reproduced on this kerchief.

Hewson's textile firm was established in 1774 under the patronage of Benjamin Franklin. A strong supporter of domestic manufactures, Franklin had brought the captain's establishment to the attention of the Washingtons. Given Hewson's bold defiance of the British ban on textile printing in the colonies, it seems only fitting that he supplied what Martha Washington conceived of as a tool for boosting the morale of the Continental Army. She is said to have ordered the kerchiefs to distribute among the troops during her frequent visits to camp. In addition to cheering the soldiers, the kerchiefs may have also been used for bundling supplies, or as headbands, bandages, slings, or masks on the battlefield.

The New-York Historical Society owns a number of kerchiefs depicting the historical figure of Washington. Produced between 1775 and the mid-twentieth century, they signal the continuing appeal of the founding father to successive generations of Americans. Other kerchiefs commemorating the War of 1812, the Civil War, and World Wars I and II are also housed in the collection, as are kerchiefs rallying support for presidential candidates from Andrew Jackson to Dwight D. Eisenhower. An informal and inexpensive means of promoting candidates and commemorating historical figures and events, these ephemeral objects serve as an vivid index to American popular culture.

Unearthing New York's History
with Pick and Shovel

IN THE 1880S, William Louis Calver (1859-1940) began scouring the northern tip of Manhattan for Native American artifacts. While combing the orchard of the Dyckman Farm, the archeologist and historian found, in the company of some arrow points, a button from the coat of a British Army soldier, unearthed by heavy rains. This surface discovery lead to an organized excavation of the site that would lay bare a history of habitation that had largely gone unrecorded.

With the help of fellow archeologist Reginald Pelham Bolton (1856-1942), Calver began excavating Revolutionary War camps centered around Fort Washington, which dated from 1776 to 1783. By studing the details of military maps and soldiers' journals, the men were able to pinpoint the locations of unexplored sites and, with the help of a volunteer force of antiquarians and amateur archeologists, began excavating with pick and shovel. Buried beneath the hillsides of Washington Heights they found evidence of successive military occupations by the Continental Army and British, loyalist, and Hessian troops. In 1918, Bolton, Calver, and their group officially organized themselves into the Field Exploration Committee of the New-York Historical Society, expanding their investigations as far as the Canadian border in order to trace the movement of troops throughout New York during the Revolutionary War and the War of 1812.

On the Dyckman Farm, Bolton and Calver uncovered sixty of an estimated one hundred and twenty, twelve-by-fifteen-foot dugouts once built on the site. Inside one of them, they found this small clay cylinder with bulbous ends. A very rare survival, this everyday object was used to curl the wig of a British or Hessian officer, or possibly the wig of an officer's wife.

Wigs featured prominently in both men and women's hairstyles during the 1770s and early 1780s. Officers favored the queue—long hair, powdered and tied at the nape of the neck in a large bow, with one or two rolled curls positioned over each ear. Wigs or toupees were frequently used to achieve this style. In England, styles with suggestive names like the Wolf and the Hedgehog were favored by women. These elaborate hairdos required setting a wig with as many as six hundred individual curlers. The process of curling the wig involved rolling the hair in dampened newspaper, wrapping it around the clay curlers, and tying each curl in place with a piece of rag. Thus arranged, the wig was baked, sometimes in a baker's oven, until dry, setting the curls. As the discovery of the wig curler suggests, officers and the wives who accompany them to America during the Revolution maintained the rituals of their social class—including their grooming habits— even in the face of war.

The job of curling a wig ideally fell to an officer's attendant. Some British officers selected soldiers from the ranks to serve as uniformed personal servants, or batmen, while others chose civilians—either family members, friends, or slaves. In garrison or on campaigns, servants relieved their employers of domestic chores by attending to their gear, meals,

WIG CURLER *from the Revolutionary period, excavated in Washington Heights by Bolton and Calver. INV. 5924.77*

and quarters. If an officer was lucky, his servant could dress hair, which was considered by many to be an irksome task. (British officers actually sought out servants with this skill: in June of 1778 and May of 1779, Rivington's *Royal Gazette*, a royalist newspaper in New York, ran advertisements on behalf of officers seeking attendants who could dress hair.) As a last resort, officers dressed each other's hair, in a ritual of mutual grooming.

Many artifacts recovered at Fort Washington lend insight into the military history of the site: cannon balls, grapeshot, bayonets, stirrups and bridle bits, apothecaries' weights, cocked hats, and badges round out historians' knowledge of Revolutionary War history. But equally fascinating are the insights gleaned from domestic objects like this wig curler. Pothooks, shovels, scissors, keys, silverware, rum bottles, razors, clay pipes, seals, and cuff links, all found at this site, evidence the mundane aspects of everyday life carried out by officers, soldiers, and camp followers. Also discovered among the relics in Washington Heights were toys—marbles, doll fragments, and camp-made dominoes— that document the presence of children in the camp. These personal artifacts offer an extraordinary glimpse into the private life that accompanied military service.

WILLIAM CALVER *of the Field Exploration Committee, pictured in a hut once occupied by the 17th Regiment of Foot of the British Army in June of 1915. Print Room, Pictorial Archive, #35703*

By the time the Field Exploration Committee disbanded in 1937, it had exposed the rich temporal layering of the site in Washington Heights. Dutch tile fragments, ceramics, and building materials looted from nearby colonial farmhouses were found within the camp, as were Native American artifacts dating from 1500 to 1700. These items suggest complex relationships between the site's former inhabitants. Bolton and Calver's artifacts now form the bulk of the New-York Historical Society's archeological collections and shed new light not only on the military history of New York, but on the daily lives of its occupants.

Pipe Dreams

AFTER LITTLE MORE than a hundred years of settlement on Manhattan Island, the water supply had become a serious problem. By the mid-eighteenth century, water from the city's wells was noxious and unsuitable for drinking. The only notable exception was the "tea water" well fed by Collect Pond, near today's Chatham and Roosevelt streets. Tea water could be purchased directly at the wellhead or from "tea watermen" who carted it throughout the city. With the city's health depending more on its water than on the rest of its food and drink combined, the move was on to find an abundant, pure, and wholesome source.

In 1799, public officials and private investors chartered the Manhattan Water Company. An outgrowth of a project initiated in 1774 by Irish immigrant engineer Christopher Colles, the group proposed to erect a reservoir within the city and carry water to every street and lane through a system of wooden pipes. With a series of perpendicular pipes laid at hundred-yard intervals, water could be drawn from convenient locations by anyone, at any time, day or night. In case of fire, conduit pipes would "communicate" with fire engines, allowing a speedy and plentiful supply of water. Postponed by the Revolutionary War, Colles' scheme was revived through an act of legislation after the war ended. A call went out for pitch pine logs, straight and free from large knots, twenty feet long and twelve inches in diameter. This cross-section of a wooden water pipe, on display in the Luce Center, is taken from one of those logs, laid in New York City sometime between 1800 and 1840 by the Manhattan Water Company. A flat, wedge-shaped piece of iron with an eyelet at the top func-tioned as a water gate, which controlled the flow of water through the pipe.

Although the charter of the Manhattan Water Company gave it the right "to erect any dams or other works across or upon any stream or streams of water, river or rivers" in order to obtain an ample supply of clean water for the city, the waterworks never availed itself of that privilege. Instead, it sank a large well twenty-five feet in diameter where Reade and Centre streets meet today and pumped the water into a reservoir on Chambers Street. The reservoir's water soon developed quality problems, and complaints about the entire enterprise mounted as New Yorkers discovered that the water mains reached only a portion of the city's residents. The project was denounced as a failure.

New York's population continued to grow rapidly during the first half of the nineteenth century and, in response to the increased risk of fire and disease, additional sources of water were investigated. Gradual improvements took shape, with iron water mains replacing wooden ones in 1833, and reservoirs replacing wells. With the completion of the Croton Aqueduct in 1842, which brought seventy-two million gallons of water a day into New York City, New Yorkers could finally boast of indoor plumbing and reliable fire hydrants. In 1917, the Catskill Aqueduct supplanted the Croton; that summer, this wooden water pipe was unearthed from the street in front of the Fraunces Tavern. It was presented to the New-York Historical Society a year later, by Abraham S. Post.

Section of WATER PIPE *laid in New York City between 1800 and 1840 by the Manhattan Water Company. X.47*

A Banner Celebration

PEWTERER'S BANNER (*detail*), *from the Federal Procession of 1788. Gift of James S. Haring, 1903.12*

BY JULY 23, 1788, the citizens of New York could no longer contain their patriotic ardor. At eight o'clock that morning, five thousand citizens—a quarter of the city's population—gathered in "The Fields" (near today's City Hall Park) and formed a procession to celebrate the ratification of the Federal Constitution by the requisite number of states. At the sounding of the gun, the mile-and-a-half-long column of men marched slowly and majestically along Broadway to Bowling Green, turned north, and passed through Hanover Square on its way to Broome Street. After feasting in the orchard of Peter Bayard and drinking to the health of the new nation, the marchers retraced their steps through the city. The fact that the New York assembly, then meeting in Poughkeepsie, had not yet added its signature to the Constitution (the cause of the month-long delay in the celebration) did not seem to dampen the spirits of either the celebrants or the onlookers, who lined the entire parade route.

The Federal Procession, organized by the General Committee of Mechanics in the City of New York, was the first parade of any magnitude in the city. Men of all classes and professions joined in the festivities, forming ten symbolic divisions (one for each state that had ratified the Constitution by that date). Foresters, farmers, millers, brewers, and artisans of every kind marched alongside merchants, traders, lawyers, university members, and foreigners of distinction. William J. Elsworth (1746-1814), who represented the Pewterer's guild at a meeting of the General Committee, presumably carried this banner made of painted orange silk for the Society of Pewterers.

Guildsmen created imaginative floats and banners that reinforced their support for the formation of a new union and celebrated the process by which it had been achieved. The bakers' float, for example, carried four master bakers who worked together to create the "federal loaf." When completed, the ten-foot-long bread bore the names of the ratifying states and the initials of those that had not yet ratified.

Many of the elements painted on the Pewterers' banner endorsed the ratification of the Constitution and formation of the new union, some more overtly than others. The image of the Pewterers' workshop painted on the guild's banner arguably functions in a similar way. Four figures representing different branches of the trade are shown at work making pewter objects, the different tasks they perform over time and in various locations combined into a single scene. Like the bakers' float, the pewterers' banner suggests that the collective efforts of the nation to form a more perfect union are finally reaping rewards. An American flag with thirteen stars—one for each state in the new union—occupies the upper left corner. Below is the Pewterers' coat of arms with the motto, "SOLID AND PURE." Like this motto, the inscription in the upper right of the banner expresses the hopes of the pewterer's guild for the new nation. It reads, "The Federal Plan Most Solid & Secure / Americans Their Freedom Will Ensure / All Arts Shall Flourish in Columbia's Land / And All Her Sons Join as One Social Band."

Collectively, these lively floats and banners sent a clear message of support for ratification of the Constitution to Pougheepsie. Whether they influenced the outcome is unknown, but the day after the parade, the delegates at the New York Convention voted thirty to twenty-seven in favor of ratification.

SOLID AND PURE,

The Federal Plan Most Solid & Secure
Americans Their Freedom Will Ensure
All Arts shall Flourish in Columbias Land
And All her Sons Join as One Social Band

SOCIETY of PEWTERERS

PEWTERER'S BANNER, *from the Federal Procession of 1788. Gift of James S. Haring, 1903.12*

THE IDEA FOR a badge signifying an officer's participation in the War of Independence took form in 1776, long before the Revolutionary War had ended. As later recounted by Thomas Jefferson, the concept was born in New York State. General George Washington and Colonel Henry Knox met up with John Adams in a tavern that year. Adams and Knox began discussing contemporary events and their corollaries in Roman history. Knox remarked that he wanted "some ribbon to wear in his hat, or in his button hole, to be transmitted to his descendants as a badge and a proof that he had fought in defense of their liberties."

This gold and enamel badge, from 1802, grew out of Knox's 1776 idea. The badge was issued to denote membership in the Society of the Cincinnati, a group made up of officers who had served in the American Revolution. Membership in the society was hereditary, and badges like this one were, as Knox had hoped, passed down from father to eldest son.

Major Pierre L'Enfant (1755-1825) designed the badge in 1783, following models established centuries earlier by European military orders. Its shape is taken from the American bald eagle, the newly chosen symbol for the United States seal. Based on Knox's original idea, the badge also depicts the Roman general Cincinnatus, the legendary model of patriotism who left his plow in the field to lead his army to victory. The badge was suspended from a deep-blue ribbon edged in white, symbolizing solidarity with the French who had fought in the Revolution.

The first badges were die-cut in Paris in 1784 and distributed to Revolutionary War officers. American silversmiths reproduced the

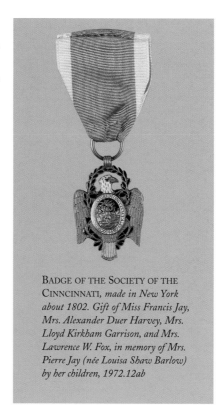

BADGE OF THE SOCIETY OF THE CINNCINNATI, *made in New York about 1802. Gift of Miss Francis Jay, Mrs. Alexander Duer Harvey, Mrs. Lloyd Kirkham Garrison, and Mrs. Lawrence W. Fox, in memory of Mrs. Pierre Jay (née Louisa Shaw Barlow) by her children, 1972.12ab*

design as new badges were needed. A New York silversmith, John Cook, began producing his version of the badge around 1802. This badge was originally owned by Matthew Clarkson (1758-1825), a soldier and first-generation member of the Society of the Cincinnati who, following the war, served as brigadier-general and then as major-general of the New York State Militia. It is one of only five known examples made by Cook.

Many members of the Society of the Cincinnati, including Clarkson, wore their eagles proudly, considering it a sign of their noble service. But outside the group, the badge was seen as symbolizing something else entirely. A society composed of the nation's most powerful military officers (and French officers, who had been allowed to join) and which maintained restrictive membership qualifications was viewed as elitist and aristocratic. This view was only encouraged by the badges, which resembled those of foreign military orders usually reserved for the nobility. The society founded by the nation's first freedom-fighters was considered a threat to republican values.

According to historians, the goals of the organization were much less sinister; they included providing charitable assistance to the families of needy officers and maintaining friendships formed among the officers during the war. But bowing to public criticism, the Society of the Cincinnati, under the leadership of President General George Washington, voted to eliminate hereditary membership in 1784. Although this change was never actually implemented, subsequent generations—with less intimate connections to the Revolutionary past—failed to join, and the

A Fête for Lafayette

GLOVE, TIARA AND FAN, *all worn to Lafayette's Ball in 1824. Gift of Samuel V. Hoffman, 1929.46; Purchased by the Society, 1920.11; Gift of Mr. A. Gordon Norrie, in the name of Eloise Lawrence Breese, 1921.14, respectively*

IN 1824, THE Marquis de Lafayette (1757-1834) returned to the United States for a firsthand look at the nation he had fought to found some forty years earlier. Gratitude for the service of one of the Revolutionary War's last surviving generals was undiminished, and on September 14, New York hosted an elaborate subscription ball to express it.

The magnificent fête took place in the amphitheater of Castle Garden under an awning of white sailcloth. Welcome banners and busts of America's elder statesmen decorated the walls. As an orchestra played, six thousand guests danced in the glow of the colored gas lights. The sixty-seven-year-old guest of honor stayed until two o'clock in the morning.

Dressed in their finest formal attire, ladies arrived in black or white satin gowns, their hair adorned with combs and ostrich plumes in the style of the day. One guest wore this tiara made in England between 1820 and 1824 out of cut steel, formed into studs and faceted to resemble gem stones. The piece was part of a suite that included a necklace, drop earrings, bracelets, shoulder ornaments, and a clasp, all worn to the ball.

A "Miss Bogert" carried this brisé fan made in Paris between 1775 and 1790 and featuring an engraving of Lafayette alongside Marie Antoinette and an allegorical figure of French patriotism. Other guests donned items custom-made for the ball. These elbow-length kid gloves decorated with a portrait of Lafayette were worn by a Miss Buddy.

Countless other items were produced for and, no doubt, worn to this event and the many others held in celebration of Lafayette's year-long visit. Jewelers offered Lafayette medals and scent bottles, dry goods stores stocked Lafayette ribbons, and milliners sold Lafayette stockings and petticoats. Many of these items have made their way into museums and historical societies throughout the country, where they serve as reminders of an episode in patriotic fanaticism and fancy. The objects illustrated here were all acquired by the New-York Historical Society around the centennial of Lafayette's return.

Civil Disobedience

IN 1863, AFTER calls for ever-increasing numbers of Northern volunteers had exhausted the supply, President Abraham Lincoln (1809-1865) resorted to the draft. Congress passed the National Conscription Act on March 3, authorizing government agents to enroll all able-bodied men between the ages of twenty and forty-five; draftees would be chosen by lottery to fight against the Confederacy.

By summer, draft wheels like this one were turning in every congressional district in New York City. This particular wheel was used on July 13, in the lottery held in the Seventh Congressional District on the Lower East Side. When given to the New-York Historical Society in 1865, one hundred cards bearing the names of men who were never drafted were still inside the drum.

Those men whose names were drawn, however, did not necessarily fight. They had two means of exempting themselves from service. One was to hire a substitute; the other was to pay a three-hundred dollar fee—a prohibitively large sum for working-class men. Before long, the slogan "rich man's war, but poor man's fight" became a powerful tool in the hands of Democrats, who made conscription into a partisan and class issue. Democratic-leaning newspapers claimed that the draft would force white working men to fight for the freedom of blacks, who would inevitably come north *en masse* and compete for jobs. Such rhetoric inflamed already smoldering racial, ethnic, and political tensions within the city population. New York's large Irish contingent was already suffering from competition created by freed black slaves and was hostile toward the Protestant middle and upper classes; Governor Horatio Seymour's own opposition to the Conscription Act practically gave them his tacit approval to revolt against a war waged by Yankee Protestants for black freedom.

On the morning of July 13, as the selection process started up at a conscription office at

DRAFT WHEEL *used in New York during the Civil War. Gift of C. Frederic Wagner, 1865.6*

Third Avenue and 46th Street, a pistol shot rang out. A crowd chanting "Down with the rich men!" hurled bricks and set fire to the building, setting off the worst urban riot in the nation's history.

For four days straight, men and women took to the streets. They tore up railroad tracks and cut telegraph wires. They torched Protestant churches and the homes of prominent Republicans and abolitionists, and then prevented firemen from putting them out. Six African Americans were lynched and thousands of others beaten. The city's seventy thousand rioters left 105 people dead and the city in shambles.

Twenty thousand federal troops called in from Gettysburg restored an uneasy peace to the city on July 17. Although the draft lottery resumed two days later, the City Council had by then appropriated funds to pay the commutation fees of drafted New Yorkers, insuring that any man whose name was drawn would not be forced to fight.

A Final Farewell

ON SATURDAY, APRIL 15, 1865, the terrible news of President Abraham Lincoln's assassination arrived on the heels of celebrations that the Civil War was won. Upon hearing the announcement, Walt Whitman took the ferry from Brooklyn to Manhattan to mourn the loss of the Great Emancipator alongside his fellow New Yorkers. The poet found the city and its people shrouded in black. The thousands of flags that ordinarily animated Broadway hung at half-mast, long black pennants obscuring their bright colors. Some time around midday it began to rain. Looking skyward, Whitman saw "black clouds…long broad black like great serpents slowly undulating in every direction." He sensed "a strange mixture of horror, fury, tenderness, and a stirring wonder brewing" at the sudden loss of the nation's leader.

That "stirring wonder" brought New Yorkers together—and out into the streets. Lincoln's body arrived in New York on April 24, en route from Washington, D.C., to its final resting place in Springfield, Illinois. From the ferry terminal at Desbrosses Street, Lincoln's cortege proceeded to City Hall, where his body, dressed in black with a white turned-down collar and white gloves, laid in state from one o'clock in the afternoon until noon the next day. A banner declaring "The Nation Mourns" draped City Hall; the rotunda was covered in national and state flags, each hemmed with black. Thousands of mourners wearing black crepe arm bands crowded City Hall Park and waited patiently in line to view the body. Boats from Brooklyn and Jersey City delivered throngs of men, women, and children throughout the night.

The line outside City Hall inched forward. The crowds stayed on, even as their hope of reaching the rotunda dwindled. Those who were lucky enough to reach the front of the line were ushered rapidly past Lincoln's body. One newspaper reported that occasionally, some daring person would attempt to touch Lincoln's face, causing soldiers of the Seventh Regiment—whose duty it was to guard the body from harm—to quickly step in. Many mourners felt compelled to leave the scene with a keepsake: people removed pieces of silver lace and fringe from the rotunda's decorations. This spray of laurel, taken by one Jeremiah Wood, is said to have lain on President Lincoln's heart while he lay in state in City Hall. Placed in a gilded frame together with a small photograph of Lincoln and a black and white crossed ribbon, this memento was given to the New-York Historical Society by a descendant of Wood in 1947.

On April 25, before a million mourners, sixteen gray horses led the funeral cortege up Broadway to the Hudson River Railroad Depot. The head of the procession reached the railroad station at about two o'clock, and at four, the train bearing Lincoln's body left the station for Albany. An hour later, the small group of African Americans that had been allowed to bring up the rear of the procession was still below 14th Street. They had been allowed to join the over sixty-thousand marchers as a last-minute compromise; the Common Council of New York had originally excluded blacks from joining the procession altogether. It was a sad and ironic moment. The war fought for the freedom of America's slaves had ended, but the fight for civil rights had hardly begun.

FLOWER FROM LINCOLN'S BIER, *framed with a photograph of the President. Gift of Mrs. Georgine Wood Charlton, Z.2603*

A scene on the ERIE CANAL *from about the 1840s. Gift of Mr. Charles E. Dunlap, 1948*

The Wedding of the Waters

THIS SMALL OAK barrel was used by Governor De Witt Clinton (1769-1828) to marry the waters of Lake Erie and the Atlantic Ocean, in celebration of the completion of the Erie Canal. The culmination of a ten-day celebration, the "marriage" took place on October 26, 1825, following a long series of festivities along the entire length of the 363-mile canal. A flotilla led by Governor Clinton had made its way from Buffalo to Albany, where it was joined by a fleet of steamships that towed the canal boats down the Hudson River to New York. Boats of every kind joined the aquatic procession in the port of New York and then floated on to Sandy Hook, where, in front of throngs of enthusiastic supporters, Clinton poured the contents of this barrel into the ocean.

For Clinton—the principal champion of the project and overseer of its construction— the celebration was personal. In 1810 he and six other commissioners had studied the feasibility of a man-made canal linking the Great Lakes to the Hudson River. Unable to drum up national support for the project, Clinton made the case for state sponsorship. In 1816, the New York State legislature adopted his plan.

Clinton had also outlined the main engineering features that the project would require— a considerable challenge, since in order to permit the continuous flow of Lake Erie's water eastward, the canal would have to breach hundred-foot changes in elevation as it passed through the Mohawk Gateway in western New York. The result was a system of eighty-three locks, which would lift and lower boats a total of over six-hundred feet. A major technological achievement, Clinton's "big ditch" inspired spectacular public celebration.

But with the marrying of the waters, the public also celebrated the anticipated profits that the project would bring. Clinton and other advocates had long predicted the commercial benefits of the Erie Canal to the state of New York and to the nation; the commercial promise of connecting upstate New York and New York City to the American West was obvious.

Residents of the state did not have to wait long to experience these profits themselves. The very construction of the Grand Canal had already given birth to more than one city upstate and had nurtured others pre-dating the canal. By the time the project was completed, life in upstate New York had been altered forever. The Erie Canal had opened a passageway to the western frontier—to Minnesota, Wisconsin, Michigan, and beyond—and settlers soon took advantage of it. Merchants followed, with all of the manufactured goods necessary to set up house on the frontier. In exchange, western settlers sent back grain and produce via the canal, both for distribution in the East and shipment to international markets through the port of New York. The canal was invaluable to New York City, effectively assuring its dominance over New Orleans as the center of trade in the eastern United States.

The Erie Canal fulfilled its promise. The seven-million-dollar project paid for itself within ten years of its construction. Although it went into decline with the introduction of railroads in the region in the 1850s, it experienced a rebirth when it became part of the expanded New York State barge canal system in the early twentieth century. The waters of Lake Erie and the Atlantic remain married: the canal still operates today.

OAK BARREL *used to ceremoniously mix the waters of Lake Erie with those of the Atlantic Ocean in 1825. X.48*

FIRE ENGINE CONDENSER CASE *from 1830–40. Purchased from Elie Nadelman, 1937.1631*

A Case for De Witt Clinton

THIS FIRE ENGINE condenser case was spotted in New York City's grand, five-mile-long procession celebrating the opening of the Croton Aqueduct in 1842. Elaborately painted, carved, and gilded, the case was mounted on the yellow truck of Clinton Engine Company No. 41, which was drawn through the parade by fifty-five firemen outfitted in their traditional fire-caps, red shirts, and dark pants. Like the ambitious aqueduct project itself, the fire company—with its bold red- and gilt-striped engine and its brave volunteers—was an object of tremendous civic pride, encouraged in no small part by the efforts of the company's namesake, De Witt Clinton (1769-1828).

Engine Company No. 41, formed in 1813, took its official name from one of the most powerful politicians of the time, who enjoyed ten one-year terms as Mayor of New York City. By the time the emblem was painted on this compressor case, Clinton had also served four times as Governor of the state and had earned New York's respect for an impressive range of accomplishments, some of which are commemorated on the condenser case itself.

The center of the emblem features a portrait bust of Clinton, with the Genius of Agriculture placing a wreath of flowers on his head. An avid naturalist, Clinton had caused a mild sensation throughout the scientific world in the 1820s when he discovered a species of wheat growing wild near Utica. Wheat had never been traced to any native location other than the shores of the Caspian Sea—generating the theory that central Asia was the cradle of civilization. Clinton's discovery of native wheat in upstate New York cast doubt on that claim, leading some to infer that New York State was the progenitor of Asia and Europe. To the right of these figures is a distant view of Albany, Clinton's home during his stints as Governor. Albany was also the eastern terminus of the Erie Canal (featured on the left), which is considered to be Clinton's crowning achievement. He was the canal's chief planner and most steadfast

promoter; in linking the Great Lakes with the Atlantic Ocean via the Hudson River, "Clinton's ditch" helped to turn New York into a world-class commercial center.

The metropolis had grown in size as well as economic importance during the first three decades of the nineteenth century, and Clinton had also had a hand in shaping New York City's changing landscape. He helped to guide the vision of the logical, right-angled grid of streets and broad avenues that would extend the city northward above Houston Street. The city's rapid expansion brought increased risks of fire and disease, however. New fire engine companies were founded in response, and the city engineered new systems for water delivery, including cisterns, reservoirs, iron water mains, and hydrants. A joint committee of the Common Council on Fire and Water engaged none other than De Witt Clinton to investigate new and abundant sources of water, and the Croton Water project was founded to divert water from the Croton River into Manhattan, providing a permanent and inexhaustible supply to the city. Although he did not live to see either the construction or the opening of the Croton Aqueduct, the volunteers of Clinton Engine Company No. 41 saw to it that De Witt Clinton was part of the celebration.

Detail of a GOOSENECK FIRE ENGINE, *from a certificate of membership issued to Sam Parker by the New York City Volunteer Fire Department on July 7, 1838. Print Room, Certificate File*

Dressed for Defense

AT THE OPENING of World War II, German U-boats sank tons of ships near the entrance to New York harbor. The threat of bloodshed on American soil spurred thousands of frightened New Yorkers to sign on with the Civilian Defense Volunteers Organization. Founded in May of 1941 by an executive order of President Franklin Delano Roosevelt, the U.S. Office of Civilian Defense (OCD) was headed up by New York Mayor Fiorello H. La Guardia until 1942. By the end of World War II, over four hundred thousand New Yorkers had suited up and served.

Mrs. John Adikes of Jamaica Estates, Long Island, was among the many women who volunteered their services to the New York City branch of the OCD. Her dress uniform, held in the New-York Historical Society's collection, consisted of a single-breasted medium-blue wool coat and matching skirt, made in New York by Saks Fifth Avenue. A blue hat with visor and chin strap, a white cotton shirt, navy tie, oxfords, and beige stockings would have completed the outfit. Insignia on the jacket's left shoulder would have identified Mrs. Adikes as a member of the Staff Corps of the OCD in the parades and other public functions she attended in New York between 1942 and 1945.

The duties performed by Mrs. Adikes would have depended upon the branch to which she belonged. Half of OCD members were assigned to the U.S. Citizens Defense Corps and charged with defending the home front, both from saboteurs and from enemy attacks by air, sea, and land. Members of this branch of the OCD served as air raid wardens, nurses' aides, auxiliary police, and fire watchers. In addition, they were organized into Demolition and Clearance Crews trained to clear the rubble from damaged buildings and to raze unsafe

ones. Decontamination Squads prepared for neutralizing contamination by "blister gases," and solitary aircraft spotters perched high on rooftops and signal towers to keep watch against invading planes. Members of the Citizens Defense Corps are perhaps best-remembered, however, for conducting periodic blackout drills and for testing air-raid sirens on Saturdays at noon.

The second branch of the OCD, the Citizens Service Corps, led "the fight against inefficiency, insecurity, and poor health" within their local communities. Its membership was entrusted with safeguarding morale, providing recreation, education, and child care, ensuring public health, and directing social and housing

> *"No better means of strengthening such a united national spirit could be imagined than by urging every American to share in the responsibilities and work of national defense through voluntary defense service, through community effort."*
>
> —Mary Steele Ross,
> *American Women in Uniform*, 1943

programs for defense industry workers and the armed forces. Block leaders ran salvage drives and promoted the conservation of commodities vital to the war effort, like rubber, gasoline, fuel oil, meat, and scrap metal.

Women served in every capacity of the OCD. Their volunteer participation helped to "bind the hearts and purposes of the men and women of the United States in a united effort." In bolstering a sense of national pride, their efforts contributed to victory abroad. Women also served in some branches of the military such as the WAVES, which organized women for volunteer emergency service as reserve midshipmen in the U.S. Navy. Similarly, the Women's Reserve of the Coast Guard, or SPARS, employed women as aviation machinists' mates, draftsmen, electricians' mates, financial assistants, gunners' mates, legal assistants, and radio operators. Examples of the uniforms of the WAVES and SPARS are also housed in collection of the Historical Society; together with this Civilian Defense uniform, they help document the significant contribution American women made to the national war effort during World War II.

The CIVIL DEFENSE VOLUNTEER ORGANIZATION UNIFORM *of Mrs. John Adikes, from 1942–45. Gift of the Mayor's Committee, 1946.89a–c*

For Further Reading

Blaugrund, Annette, and Theodore Stebbins, Jr., eds., *John James Audubon: The Watercolors for Birds of America*, 1st ed. (New York: Random House and the New-York Historical Society, 1994).

Bonomi, Patricia U., *The Lord Cornbury Scandal: The Politics of Reputation in British America* (Chapel Hill: University of North Carolina Press for the Omohundro Institute of Early American History and Culture, Williamsburg, 1998).

Breton, Arthur J., *A Guide to the Manuscript Collections of the New-York Historical Society* (Westport, Conn.: Greenwood Press, 1972).

Burrows, Edwin G., and Mike Wallace, *Gotham: A History of New York City to 1898* (New York and Oxford: Oxford University Press, 1999).

Da Costa Nunes, Jadviga M., and Ferris Olin, *Baroness Hyde de Neuville: Sketches of America, 1807-1822* (New Brunswick, N.J., and New York: Jane Voorhees Zimmerli Art Museum, Rutgers, State University of New Jersey, and the New-York Historical Society, 1984).

Foshay, Ella M., *Mr. Luman Reed's Picture Gallery: A Pioneer Collection of American Art* (New York: Harry N. Abrams, 1990).

Groce, George C., and David H. Wallace, *The New-York Historical Society's Dictionary of Artists in America, 1564-1860* (New Haven and London: Yale University Press and Oxford University Press, 1957).

Guthrie, Kevin M., *The New-York Historical Society: Lessons From One Nonprofit's Long Struggle for Survival* (San Francisco: Jossey-Bass, 1996).

Jackson, Kenneth T., and the New-York Historical Society, *The Encyclopedia of New York City* (New Haven and New York: Yale University Press and the New-York Historical Society, 1995).

Koke, Richard J., et al., *American Landscape and Genre Paintings in the New-York Historical Society: A Catalog of the Collection* (Boston: G.K. Hall in association with the New-York Historical Society, 1982).

Lamb, Martha J., *History of the City of New York: Its Origin, Rise, and Progress* 2 vols. (New York: A. S. Barnes and Co., 1877-80).

Leighton, Roberta, *History Written with Pick and Shovel: Military Buttons, Belt-Plates, Badges, and Other Relics Excavated From Colonial, Revolutionary, and War of 1812 Camp Sites by the Field Exploration Committee of the New-York Historical Society* (New York: The New-York Historical Society, 1950).

Miller, Lillian B., *Patrons and Patriotism: The Encouragement of the Fine Arts in the United States, 1770-1860* (Chicago: University of Chicago Press, 1966).

Neustadt, Egon, *The Lamps of Tiffany* (New York: The Fairfield Press, 1970).

The New-York Historical Society, *Catalogue of American Portraits in the New-York Historical Society* (New Haven: Yale University Press for the New-York Historical Society, 1974).

Orosz, Joel J., *Curators and Culture: The Museum Moment in America, 1740-1870* (Tuscaloosa: University of Alabama Press, 1990).

Stokes, I. N. Phelps, *The Iconography of Manhattan Island, 1498-1909* (Mansfield, Conn.: Martino Fine Books, Union, N.J.: Lawbook Exchange, 1998).

Vail, R. W. G., *Knickerbocker Birthday: A Sesqui-Centennial History of the New-York Historical Society, 1804-1954* (New York: The New-York Historical Society, 1954).

Wallace, David W., *John Rogers: The People's Sculptor* (Middletown, Conn.: Wesleyan University Press, 1967).

Zinkham, Helena, *A Guide to Print, Photograph, Architectural and Ephemera Collections at the New-York Historical Society* (New York: The New-York Historical Society, 1998).

List of Figures

ALL WORKS ILLUSTRATED in this book are held in the museum or library collections of the New-York Historical Society. The dimensions of works of art are listed with height preceding width. In the case of three-dimensional objects, those dimensions are followed by depth.

Introduction

Pages iv-1
Map of lower New York City with vignettes marking the locations and illustrating the façades of the New-York Historical Society's buildings, detail, ca. 1954. Print Room, Pictorial Archives, #37725

Page 3
Map of lower New York City with vignettes marking the locations and illustrating the façades of the New-York Historical Society's buildings between 1804 and 1908, ca. 1954. Print Room, Pictorial Archives, #37725

Page 4
The New-York Gallery of the Fine Arts, the New-York Historical Society, Second Avenue, after 1867, photograph. Print Room, Pictorial Archives, #198

Page 7
Reading Room of the library, second floor of the New-York Historical Society, 170 Central Park West, about 1950. Print Room, Pictorial Archives, #7284

Page 8
Furniture Installation, the Henry Luce III Center for the Study of American Culture at the New-York Historical Society. Photograph courtesy of Alan Orling, September 2000.

Paintings, Miniatures and Works on Paper

Page 12
John Wollaston (active 1742-1775), *William Walton* (1706-1768), ca. 1750, oil on linen, 51 x 41 in. Bequest of Theodora M. Storm, 1902.3

Page 13
John Wollaston (active 1742-1775), *Mrs. William Walton* (1708-1786), ca. 1750, oil on linen, 51 x 41 in. Bequest of Theodora M. Storm, 1902.4

Page 14
Commission issued by Queen Anne of England on December 5, 1702, to Lord Cornbury, as Governor of the Province of New York. Library, Manuscript Department, Lord Cornbury Papers, #522A

Page 15
Unidentified artist, *Edward Hyde, Lord Cornbury* (1702-08), oil on linen, 50 x 39 in. Purchased by the Society, 1952.80

Page 16
F. Bartoli (active 1783-ca. 1796), *Portait of the Seneca Chief, Cornplanter (Ki-On-Twog-Ky)* (1732/40-1836), 1796, oil on linen, 30 x 25$\frac{1}{4}$ in. Signed at right: "F. Bartoli./New York./1796." Gift of Thomas Jefferson Bryan, 1867.314

Page 18
Francis Guy (1760-1820), *The Tontine Coffee House*, ca. 1797 or possibly 1803-4, oil on linen, 43 x 65 in. Purchased by the Society, 1907.32

Page 19
Baroness Hyde de Neuville (ca. 1749-1849), *Sketch Made at the Economical School, New York City*, detail, New York, NY, 1810-14, black chalk and graphite, 7$\frac{5}{8}$ x 6 in. Purchased by the Society, 1953.274f

Page 20
Rembrandt Peale (1778-1860), *Thomas Jefferson* (1743-1826), 1805, oil on canvas, 28 x 23$\frac{1}{2}$ in. Gift of Thomas Jefferson Bryan, 1867.306

Page 21
Charles Willson Peale (1741-1827), *Self Portrait with Mastodon Bone*, 1824, oil on linen, 27 x 23 in. Purchased by the New-York Historical Society, 1940.202

Page 22
Anthony Meucci (1808-1889), *Pierre Toussaint* (1766-1853), New York, NY, ca. 1825, watercolor on ivory, 3¼ x 2⅝ in. overall. Signed at the right: "Meucci." Gift of Miss Georgina Schuyler, 1920.4

Page 23
Anthony Meucci (1808-1889), *Euphemia Toussaint* (1815-1829), New York, NY, ca. 1825, watercolor on ivory, 3⅛ x 2½ in. Gift of Miss Georgina Schuyler, 1920.6

Page 23
Anthony Meucci (1808-1889), *Mrs. Pierre Toussaint (Juliette Noel)* (ca. 1786-1851), New York, NY, ca. 1825, watercolor on ivory, 3¼ x 2⅝. Gift of Miss Georgina Schuyler, 1920.5

Page 25
John James Audubon (1785-1851), *Carolina Parakeets (Conuropais carolinensis)*, ca. 1825, watercolor, gouache, pastel, crayon, and graphite on paper, 40 x 30 in. (with mat). Inscribed in pencil (faint), lower right: "No. 6/Plate 26-"; inscribed in pencil (faint), lower left center: "Carolina Parrot-Psitacus Carolinensis"; inscribed in pencil (faint), lower center: "Males 1. F. 2. Young 3"; inscribed in pencil (faint), lower right center: "Plant Vulgo Cockle burr-The upper Specimen was shot near Bayou Sarah and appeared so uncommon having 14 Tailfeathers all 7 sizes distinct and firmly affixed in 14 different receptacles that I drew it more to verify one of those astonishing fits of Nature than any thing else—it was a female. The Green Headed (a young bird) is also a singular although not so uncommon Variety as the above one—Louisiana-December—J. J. Audubon." Purchased for the Society by public subscription from Mrs. John J. Audubon, 1863.17.26

Pages 26-27, 28
Thomas Cole (1801-1848), *The Course of Empire: The Consummation of Empire*, 1835-36, oil on canvas, 52 x 76 in. Signed and dated, right center: "T. Cole / 1836"; on a label attached to reverse of

original wood panel, written in the artist's hand: "The picture with the four others constitute a Series called the Course of Empire. They were painted for Mr. Luman Reed of N. York; but I had to lament his death before the work was completed—in him I lost a noble friend & the Fine Arts a true lover and liberal patron— / Thomas Cole / Cedar Grove / Near Catskill / Sept 29th 1836." New-York Gallery of the Fine Arts, 1858.3

Pages 29, 30-31
Eastman Johnson (1824-1906), *Negro Life at the South (Old Kentucky Home)*, 1859, oil on linen, 37 x 46 in. Signed and dated, lower right: "E. Johnson / 1859." The Robert L. Stuart Collection, on permanent loan from the New York Public Library, 1944, S-225

Pages 32-33
Asher B. Durand (1796-1886), *The Solitary Oak (The Old Oak)*, 1844, oil on canvas, 37 x 49 in. Signed and dated, bottom, right of center: "A B Durand / 1844"; on old paper label on stretcher: "Landscape / A.B. Durand / New York / [ ] 6 [ ]"; painted on reverse of frame: "As Rcd. A[merican] A[rt] Union and 80." New-York Gallery of the Fine Arts, 1858.75

Pages 34-35
Edward Burckhardt (1815-1903), *Panoramic View of New York City*, panels 3 and 4, 1842-45, pen-and-ink on paper, 13 x 240 in. overall. Gift of Mrs. Harold Farquhar Hadden, 1915.76

Page 35
John Johnston (1824-1906), *New York City from the World Building*, 1894, photograph. Print Room, Geographic Files, #51228

Page 37
William Henry Burr (1819-1908), *The Intelligence Office*, 1849, oil on linen, 22 x 27 in. Signed, lower right: "W. H. Burr"; on reverse of canvas: "The Intelijuns Ofis / Wm. Henri Bur / June 1849." Purchased by the Society, 1959.46

Page 38
Thomas Hicks (1823-1890), *Elisha Kent Kane* (1820-1857), 1858, oil on linen, 42 x 52 in. Signed, lower left: "T.Hicks / 1858." Gift of several ladies of New York, 1859.1

Page 39
Jasper Francis Cropsey (1823-1900), *Castle Garden, New York*, 1859, oil on linen, 16 x 25 in. Signed and dated, bottom center: "J. F. Cropsey / 1859"; on wood backing panel, in pencil: "Castle Garden, New York / J.F. Cropsey [?] 1859." Purchased by the Society, 1972.13

Page 40
George Catlin (1796-1872), *Blackfoot Doctor (a Medicine Man)*, 1866-68, pencil and pen-and-ink on art cardboard, 18 3/8 x 24 1/8 in. Signed: "Geo. Catlin," lower right. Purchased from George Catlin, 1872.23.173

Pages 42-43
Frederic Edwin Church (1826-1900), *Cayambe*, 1858, oil on canvas, 41 1/4 x 59 3/8 in. Signed and dated, lower left (on stone block): "F. E. Church / 1858." The Robert L. Stuart Collection, on permanent loan from the New York Public Library, 1944, S-91

Pages 44-45
John Frederick Kensett (1816-1872), *Shrewsbury River, New Jersey*, 1859, oil on linen, 19 x 31 in. Signed and dated, lower left: "JFK '59." The Robert L. Stuart Collection, on permanent loan from the New York Public Library, 1944, S-229

Page 46
Carl Weidner (1865-1906) and Fredrika Weidner, *Daughters of Heber Reginald Bishop* (1840-1902), New York, NY, ca. 1895, watercolor on ivory, 3 3/4 x 3 in. Signed at right: "C. and F. Weidner." Gift of Mr. Peter Marié, 1905.22

Page 47
Cornelia Adele Fassett (1831-1898), *Mrs. Charles A. Lamb* (1829-1893), ca. 1878, oil on millboard, 15 1/4 x 24 1/4 in. Signed, lower right: "C. A. Fassett, 1878." Bequest of the subject, 1893.2

Page 49
Enit Kaufman (1897-1961), *Marian Anderson* (1897-1993), ca. 1940, watercolor over graphite on paper, 27 1/8 x 20 1/2 in. Gift of the artist, 1947.216

Page 50
Childe Hassam (1859-1935) *Flags on 57th Street, Winter 1918*, New York, NY, oil on linen, 37 x 25 in. Signed, lower right: "Childe HASSAM 1918." Bequest of Julia B. Engel (Mrs. Solton Engel), 1984.68

Sculpture

Page 54
Unidentified artist, *Death mask of Aaron Burr* (1756-1836), NY, 1836, plaster with wash, 13 1/4 x 6 1/4 x 7 1/2 in. Gift of Dr. John E. Stillwell, October 18, 1927, 1927.59

Page 55
Aaron Burr (1756-1836) to Alexander Hamilton (1756/57-1804). June 18. 1804. Library, Manuscript Department, BV Hamilton, Alexander, #73796

Page 56
Joseph Wilton (1722-1803), *William Pitt, the Elder, First Earl of Chatham* (1708-1778), ca. 1770, marble, 71 x 29 x 29 in. Inscribed on bronze plaque: "MARBLE STATUE OF WILLIAM PITT (LORD CHATHAM) / THIS STATUE WAS ERECTED BY THE COLONY OF NEW YORK SEPTEMBER 7, 1770 AT THE INTERSECTION OF WALL AND WILLIAM STREETS IT WAS MUTILATED BY THE BRITISH SOLDIERS SOON AFTER THEIR OCCUPATION OF THE CITY IN 1776. JOSEPH WILTON, SCULPTOR." Gift of Mr. Simon F. Mackie, 1864.5

Page 57
Joseph Wilton (1722-1803), *Fragment of George III statue*, England and New York, NY, 1770-76, lead with traces of gilding, 7 1/4 x 19 x 13 1/2 in. Purchased by the Society, 1878.6

Page 59
Unidentified artist, *Statue of a Fire Chief* (once thought to have been Harry Howard) (1822-1896), New York, NY, ca. 1857, polychrome painted and carved wood, 100 x 66 x 44 in. overall. Purchased from Elie Nadelman, 1937.328

Page 60
Thomas Crawford (1813-1857), *The Indian: The Dying Chief Contemplating the Progress of Civilization,* 1856, white marble and wood, 60 x 55 1/2 x 28 in. overall. Inscribed: "Presented by / Frederic De Peyster, President of the Society." Gift of Mr. Frederic De Peyster, 1875.4

Page 62
John Quincy Adams Ward (1830-1910), *The Indian Hunter,* 1860, brown patinated bronze, 16 x 14 x 10 in. overall. Signed on upper base: "J.Q.A. Ward / 1860." Gift of Mr. George A. Zabriskie, 1939.390

Page 63
Malvina Hoffman (1885-1966), *Anna Pavlova* (1885-1931), 1924, brown flesh-tone painted plaster with wooden base, 25 3/4 x 20 x 10 1/2 in. overall. Signed under left arm: "Malvina / 1924." Gift of the artist, Miss Malvina Hoffman, 1952.45

Page 65
John Rogers (1829-1904), *Checkers Up at the Farm,* New York, NY, 1877, pinkish-brown painted plaster, 20 x 17 1/4 x 11 1/4 in. overall. Signed on front of base: "JOHN ROGERS / NEW YORK"; inscribed on front of base: "CHECKERS / UP AT THE FARM"; inscribed proper left rear of base: "PATENTED / DECEMBER 28 1875." Gift of Mr. Samuel V. Hoffman, 1928.29

Page 66
Augustus Saint-Gaudens (1848-1907), *Diana of the Tower,* 1899, red-brown patinated bronze, 38 5/8 x 14 3/4 x 11 in. overall. Inscribed on front of base: "DIANA OF THE TOWER"; signed on back of base: "AUGUSTUS SAINTGAUDENS MDCCCXCIX." Purchased by the Society, 1977.3

Page 67
Madison Square Garden, 1900, photograph. Print Room, Geographic Files, #72161

Furniture

Page 70
Baby walker, probably Holland or Germany, or possibly America or U.S., 1700-1800, pine, 15 x 25 3/4 x 25 3/4 in. Inv. 14959

Page 71
Kas, the Netherlands, 1675-1700, walnut, walnut veneer, and oak, 87 x 88 1/2 x 29 in. Gift of Dr. Fenwick Beekman, 1941.914

Page 72
Designed by Jacques Gondoin (1737-1818), constructed by François II Foliot (1748-ca. 1786), *Side chair,* France, 1779, beech with gliding, 41 x 23 x 21 in. Stenciled on chair's original webbing: French royal inventory number "194" and crowned "W" of the Chateau of Versailles. Gift of Mrs. Gouverneur Morris, 1817.13

Page 73
Original webbing on the underside of *Side chair,* showing royal inventory number and marks. Conservation Files, Condition Photographs, 1986

Page 74
Dressing table, New York, NY, 1795-1810, mahogany, mahogany and other inlays, white pine, and yellow poplar, 65 1/4 x 47 x 22 in. overall. Written on lower-right hand drawer: "Livingston." Gift of Goodhue Livingston, Inv. 14982

Page 74
Plate 49, "A Lady's Cabinet Dressing Table," from Thomas Sheraton (1751-1806), *Cabinet Makers and Upholsterers Drawing Book* (London, 1793). Library Collections, #73196

Page 75
Charles-Honoré Lannuier (1779-1819), *French press,* New York, NY, 1812-19, mahogany, mahogany veneer, yellow poplar, white pine, brass, and plaster, 101 3/4 x 63 x 25 3/4 in. overall. Inscribed under plaster bust, in script: "H. Lannuier / New York." Gift of Mrs. William Hyde Wheeler, 1943.368

Page 76
Armchair, New York, NY, 1785-89, mahogany, pine, and poplar, 37³/₄ x 24¹/₂ x 21 in. overall. Engraved brass plaque on crest rail (left): "USED BY PRESIDENT U.S. GRANT/ AT HIS INAUGURATION MARCH 4, 1873"; engraved brass plaque on crest rail (center): "CHAIR USED AT THE INAUGURATION OF / GEORGE WASHINGTON / AS THE PRESIDENT OF THE UNITED STATES, APRIL 30, 1789 / PRESENTED BY EDMUND B. SOUTHWICK / MARCH 7, 1916"; engraved brass plaque on crest rail (right): "USED BY PRESIDENT JAMES A. GARFIELD / AT HIS INAUGURATION MARCH 4, 1881." Gift of Edmund B. Southwick, 1916.7

Page 77
Railing, New York, NY, 1788-89, iron, 37⁹/₁₆ x 70 x 1³/₄ in. Gift of the Chamber of Commerce of the State of New York, 1884.3

Page 78
Robert Fulton (1765-1815), *The Clermont*, February 2, 1808, wash drawing. Library, Manuscript Department, Robert R. Livingston Papers, #39796

Page 79
Settee, U.S., 1807-14, maple and paint, 27⁵/₈ x 81 x 21 in. Gift of Randall J. Le Boeuf, Jr., 1976. Inv. 14952

Page 80
Asher B. Durand (1796-1886) (after Gilbert Stuart), *George Washington* (1732-1799), 1835, oil on canvas, 30 x 25¹/₄. Gift of the New-York Gallery of the Fine Arts, 1858.32

Page 81
Armchair, New York, NY, 1856-57, oak, 65 x 31 x 27 in. overall. Engraved on silver plaque on rear seat rail: "This Chair / was made from timber of the house / in which GEORGE WASHINGTON resided / when first inaugurated president of the / UNITED STATES / Presented by Benjamin R. Winthrop / Nov. 3, 1857. Gift of Benjamin Robert Winthrop, 1857.11

Decorative Objects

Page 84
Evert Duyckinck (1621-1702), *Stained glass window*, 1656, glass and lead, 30¹/₂ x 27¹/₄ x 1 in. Enameled cartouche inscribed: "Bij mij Jan Ni-/claez van Perbon mole-/naer met Aeltgen Syboustdr Sijn huisjvrou tot Leijderdorp, 1614." Gift of Mrs. Howard C. Robbins, 1951.414c

Page 84
Evert Duyckinck (1621-1702), *Stained glass window*, detail, 1656, glass and lead. Inscribed: "Joris CLaesz vanderLaen / Anno 1630." Gift of Mrs. Howard C. Robbins, 1951.414b

Page 85
Benjamin Wynkoop, *Two-handled bowl*, New York, NY, ca. 1710, silver, 5³/₄ x 12³/₈ x 8³/₄ in. Engraved on lower center of one lobe: "P / C * M" in block letters; engraved on opposite lobe: "E. D. P."; engraved on center of bowl: "H. C. de Peyster" in script; stamped at lip: "W. K / B" in a heart. Bequest of Catharine Augusta De Peyster, 1911.38

Page 86
Lewis Fueter, *Salver*, NY, 1772-73, silver. 1¹/₂ X 21³/₄ in. Engraved in the center around the seal: "This Piece of Plate is the Gift of His Exely. Govr. Tryon, the Genel.: Assemy.: of New-York, to Capt. Sowers Engineer. 13 Mar.h 1773" in roman letters; engraved below the seal, in the center: "SIGILL / CIVITAT * NOV / EBORA" in roman letters; engraved on the base: "This piece of plate / was given to Captain Thomas Sowers in 1773, / who gave it to his daughter / Ann, / wife of Gilbert Aspinwall, / who gave it to her daughter, / Sarah Ann, / wife of James Lawrence Moore, / who gave it to her nephew, / James Lawrence Aspinwall, / (great grandson of Captain Thomas Sowers,) / who presented it to his wife / Mary Morris Carnochan, / on their wedding day / June 4th 1891. / James Lawrence Aspinwall / Presents this plate to / the New York Historical Society / January 17th, 1928"; stamped on the base: "L. Fueter" in script in a conforming rectangle. Gift of J. Lawrence Aspinwall, 1928.24

Page 88
Clarkson Crolius, Sr. (1773-1843), *Batter Pitcher*, 1798, stoneware, 12 x 9 in. Inscribed by hand around belly: "New York Feby 17th. 1798 / Flowered by Clarkson Crolius / Blue." Purchased from Elie Nadelman, 1937.587

Page 89
Stoneware for Sale by Clarkson Crolius, broadside, September 3, 1804. Library, Manuscripts Department, Clarkson Crolius Manuscripts, Misc. MSS Crolius, Wm F. Crolius notebook, 1827.

Page 90
Cornwall Kirkpatrick (1814-1890) and Wallace V. Kirkpatrick (1828-1896), Anna Potteries, *Jug and stopper*, Anna, Ill., 1871, stoneware, 12 1/4 x 11 1/2 in. Inscribed in rectangle near base: "From, / Kirkpatrick, / Anna Ills / Th. Nast NY." Gift of Mrs. Thomas Nast, 1906.6ab

Page 91
Thomas Nast, "Who Stole the People's Money? Do Tell. NYT," *Harper's Weekly*, August 19, 1871. Library Collections, #31110A

Page 93
Punch Bowl, France or England, 1824-40, earthenware, 23 x 32 in. Painted at bottom right of scene: "LANDING OF GEN-LAFAYETTE / at Castle Garden New York / 16th August 1824." Gift of Rosalie M. Heiser and John Jay Heiser, 1910.24

Page 94
Possibly Brooklyn Glass Works, *Compote with cover*, U.S., possibly Brooklyn, NY, ca. 1823-45, glass, 11 x 8 in. Gift of Lena Cadwalader Evans, 1936.693ab

Page 95
Possibly Brooklyn Glass Works, *Decanter and stopper*, U.S., possibly Brooklyn, NY, ca. 1823-45, glass, 8 3/4 x 3 in. Embossed on side: "WINE." Gift of Lena Cadwalader Evans, 1936.696ab

Page 95
Will of Abigail Corse, August 23, 1842. Library, Manuscript Department, Corse Papers

Page 97
Charles Grosjean (d. 1888), Tiffany & Co., *Ice Cream Dish*, New York, NY, 1877-78, silver, 6 1/4 x 15 3/8 in. Wrought applied to rim: "MLM" in foliate roman letters; stamped on the base: "TIFFANY & Co / 4878 MAKERS 5635 / STERLING-SILVER / 925-1000/ M"; engraved on the base: "207/ _ / 5." Gift of John Mackay, 1980.14

Page 98
Tiffany & Co., *Controller Handle*, New York, NY, 1904, silver and ebony, 8 1/4 x 9 1/8 x 2 7/8 in. Embossed across the top of the handle: "CONTROLLER HANDLE / USED BY / THE HON. GEORGE B. McCLELLAN, MAYOR OF THE CITY OF NEW YORK / IN STARTING THE FIRST TRAIN ON THE / RAPID TRANSIT RAILROAD FROM CITY HALL STATION / NEW YORK, THURSDAY, OCTOBER 27TH, 1904." in roman letters. Gift of George B. McClellan, 1922.103

Pages 98-99
City Hall Station, IRT Subway 1904, *Saturday Evening Mail*, November 1904. Print Room, Halftone Reproduction, #38215A

Page 99
Opening of City Hall subway station, 1903. Print Room, Negative File, #29079A

Pages 100, 101
Louis Comfort Tiffany (1848-1933), Tiffany Studios, *"Drophead Dragonfly" table lamp*, New York, NY, 1899-1920, glass and bronze, 28 x 22 in. overall. Donated by Egon Neustadt, N84.113

Tools for Home and Trade

Page 104
John Ramage (d. 1802), *Memorial sample card*,
watercolor and hair on ivory. Gift of an anonymous
donor, 1947.490a

Page 105
Slant-top desk, probably New York, 1775-95,
mahogany, 42¾ x 27¾ x 21½ in. overall. Gift
of an anonymous donor, 1947.461

Page 105
Slant-top desk (open), 1775-95, mahogany, 42¾ x
27¾ x 21½ in. overall. Gift of an anonymous
donor, 1947.461. Print Room, Negative File,
#28846c

Page 107
Probably John Conger (1803-1869), *Cake board*,
New York, NY, 1825-35, wood, 8 x 14½ x 1 in.
Carved on obverse: "MANHATTAN" above fire
engine and "8" twice on engine; carved on reverse:
"SUPERIOR" above fire engine and "17" on
engine. Purchased from Elie Nadelman, 1937.1562

Page 108
Physician's Saddlebags and Medicines, 1800-50,
leather, metal, glass, and paper, 7½ x 9½ x 9 in.
Gift of Mrs. E. L. Woolf, 1954.11

Page 109
Shackles, 1866, steel, 4¼ x 23 x ¼ in. Gift of Mrs.
Carroll Beckwith, 1921.20

Page 110
Architect's sign, wood, 40 x 25¾ x 4½ in. Painted in
gold on both sides: "JNO. B. SNOOK / Architect.
/ ESTABLISHED 1837." Gift of Thomas E.
Snook, Jr., 1953.197

Page 111
Reade Street elevation drawing for the A. T.
Stewart Store, 1859. Print Room, John B. Snook
Architectural Record Collection, #53487

Private Life and Public Service

Pages 114, 115
Wedding dress, U.S., 1712, silk brocade and needlepoint lace, 55 x 70 in. overall (31½ in. waist). Gift
of Mrs. Arthur T. Sutcliffe, 1949.115a

Page 116
Probably Walter Brind, *Chatelaine*, probably
London, England, ca. 1761, silver gilt, gold,
enamel, ivory, chalcedony, glass, and paint, 1⅛ x
4⅜ x 7⅝ in. overall. Engraved reverse of hook:
"Henry and Cornelia Remsen / M 28 Dec. 1761";
engraved reverse of miniature: "John Henry
Remsen / B 2 Aug. 1772 / D 15 Sept. 1798";
stamped reverse of hook: "WB." Gift of Mrs.
Edward Rutledge and daughters, 1954.179a-d

Page 117
*Wooden leg of Gouverneur Morris (1752-1816)
mounted on stand*, possibly U.S., 1780-1816, oak,
leather, and metal, 42½ x 14½ in. Gift of Mrs.
Frederick Menzies, 1954.148

Page 118
Grenadier Cap, Conn., 1740-70, wool and linen, 13
x 10½ x 3¾ in. overall. Embroidered top of front:
"AUT VINCE AUT MORI." Purchased by the
Society, 1890.3

Page 119
Masonic apron, U.S., 1770-1800, silk and metal,
23⅛ x 16⅛ x ⅛ in. Gift of Goodhue Livingston,
Jr., 1951.523ab

Page 120
Camp bed, U.S., 1777-85, wood, canvas, and iron,
27¾ x 78 x 34½ in. overall. Inscribed on brass
plaque affixed to inner face of headboard: "The
Camp Bedstead / used by / General Washington /
during the Revolution. / Presented to the / NEW
YORK HISTORICAL SOCIETY, / BY / Ernest
Livingston McCrackan." Gift of Ernest Livingston
McCrackan, 1871.8

Page 121
Possibly John Hewson, *Kerchief*, 1777-89,
Philadelphia, cotton, 30 x 30 in. Printed around
medallion: "GEORGE WASHINGTON, ESQ.
FOUNDATOR AND PROTECTOR OF
AMERICA'S LIBERTY AND INDEPENDENCY."
Gift of Mrs. J. Insley Blair, 1952.63

Page 122
Wig curler, U.S., England, or Germany, 1760-75, clay, 2⁷/₈ x ¹/₂ in. overall. Inv. 5924.77

Page 123
Unknown photographer, William Calver of the New-York Historical Society Field Exploration Committee, in Hut #23, the Hut Camp of the 17th Regiment of Foot of the Dyckman Farm and Seaman Ave., June 6, 1915. Print Room, Pictorial Archive, #35703

Page 124
Section of Water Pipe, 1800-40, wood and iron, 24 x 15 x 15 in. Engraved on plaque: "SECTION OF THE WATER PIPE / WITH IRON WATER GATE / LAID BY / THE MANHATTAN COMPANY," X.47

Pages 125, 126-27
Pewterer's Banner, New York, NY, 1788, silk and paint, 92 x 120 x 2³/₄ in. overall, including frame. Painted at top right: "The Federal Plan Most Sold & Secure / Americans Their Freedom Will Endure / All Art Shall Flourish in Columbia's Land / And All her Sons Join as One Social Band"; painted below shield: "SOLID AND PURE"; painted above shop image: "SOCIETY OF PEWTER-ERS." Gift of James S. Haring, 1903.12

Page 128
John Cook, *Badge of the Society of the Cincinnati*, New York, NY, about 1802, silk, gold, and enamel, 1¹/₂ x 3³/₄ in. overall. Written on reverse of enamel plaque: "SOCIETAS : CINCINNATORUM : INSTITUTA : AD : 1783"; written on obverse of enamel plaque: "OMNIA : RELINQUIT : SER-VARE : REMPUBLICAM." Gift of Miss Francis Jay, Mrs. Alexander Duer Harvey, Mrs. Lloyd Kirkham Garrison, and Mrs. Lawrence W. Fox, in memory of Mrs. Pierre Jay (née Louisa Shaw Barlow) by her children, 1972.12ab

Page 129
Glove, U.S., ca. 1824, leather, 21 x 4³/₄ in. Printed top of hand above image of Lafayette: "WELCOME LA FAYETTE THE NATIONS GUEST." Gift of Samuel V. Hoffman, 1929.46

Page 129
Tiara, England, 1820-24, cut steel and other metal, 2 x 7¹/₄ x 3¹/₄ in. overall. Purchased by the Society, 1920.11

Page 129
Brisé fan, Paris, France, ca. 1824, wood, paper, and ribbon, 18 x 11 x 1 in. open. Engraved above image of Marie Antoinette: "Marie Antoinette Reine de France, née a Vienne le 2 Nov.bre 1755"; engraved above image of Lafayette: "M. le Marquis de laFayette Commandant de la Garde Nationale Parisienne." Gift of Mr. A. Gordon Norrie, in the name of Eloise Lawrence Breese, 1921.14

Page 130
Draft Wheel, New York, NY, ca. 1863, wood and metal, 23 x 25¹/₂ x 21³/₄ in. Engraved on brass plaque: "DRAFT WHEEL / USED JULY 13, 1863 / WITH NAMES OF RESIDENTS IN THE / 7TH CONGRESSIONAL DISTRICT N.Y. CITY / COMPRISING THE 11TH AND 17TH WARDS / PRESENTED BY FREDERIC C. WAGNER / CAPTAIN AND PROVOST MARSHALL / JUNE 20TH 1865." Gift of Frederic C. Wagner, 1865.6

Page 131
Flower from Lincoln's Bier, 1865, plant material, photograph, silk, and wood with gilding. Inscribed in ink below laurel: "[Th]is laurel lay on President Lincoln's heart / while lying in state for three days in / City Hall in New York April 25th / 1865"; inscribed in pencil on reverse of frame: "Gift of Mrs. Georgine Wood Charlton / 2/11/47 / Taken from Lincoln's bier by Jeremiah Wood." Gift of Mrs. Georgine Wood Charlton, Z.2603

Page 131
Lincoln's funeral procession, detail, 1865, stereo-graph. Print Room, Pictorial Archives, Bague Collection, #60861

Page 132
Attributed to George Harvey (ca. 1800-1878), *Scene on the Erie Canal*, ca. 1840-49, oil on linen, 15¹/₂ x 20¹/₂ in. Inscribed: *Prepared / by / Theo. Kelley / rear 35—Wooster St. / New York*. Gift of Mr. Charles E. Dunlap, 1948.47

Page 133
Erie Canal Barrel, 1825, wood, metal, and paint, 16 x
12 in. Engraved on brass plaque: "KEG / FROM
WHICH GOVERNOR CLINTON / POURED
THE WATER OF LAKE ERIE INTO THE
ATLANTIC / OCTOBER 26, 1825 / ON THE
COMPLETION OF THE ERIE CANAL"; painted
on front of barrel: "WATER / Lake Erie." X.48

Page 134
Possibly Thomas Greenwell, *Fire engine condenser
case*, New York, NY, 1830-40, wood and paint with
gilding, 32 x 30¼ x 15 in. overall. Purchased from
Elie Nadelman, 1937.1631

Page 135
Certificate of membership, detail, issued to Sam
Parker by the Volunteer Fire Department, City of
New York Firemen, July 7, 1838. Print Room,
Certificate File

Page 136
J & E. Stevens Co., *Toy Mechanical Bank*, Cromwell,
Conn., 1875, iron and paint, 5¾ x 4⅜ x 3 in. Cast
on each side of chair: "TAMMANY BANK" with
fan motif at center; cast on back of chair, top:
"PATD DEC 23 1873." Purchased from Elie
Nadelman, 1937.1237

Page 137
Produced by the firm of Heinrich Handwerck
(1876-1930), dressed by Mrs. Grover Cleveland
(1864-1947), *Doll*, Gotha, Thuringia, Germany, ca.
1893, ceramic, composition, textile, leather, fur,
hair, rhinestones, feathers, and paint, 18 x 12 x 4
in. overall. Impressed on back of head: "109 / H /
1." Gift of Mrs. Katharine Prentis Murphy,
1961.31

Page 139
Saks Fifth Avenue, *Coat*, New York, NY, 1942-45,
wool, silk, and metal, 3 x 17 x 28¾ in. overall.
Embroidered maker's label, inside neck: "Saks
Fifth Avenue"; cast on the face of each button: "E
PLURIBUS UNUM"; stamped on reverse of each
button: "HANDY MACHCO / NEW YORK."
Gift of the Mayor's Committee, 1946.89a

Page 139
Saks Fifth Avenue, *Skirt*, New York, NY, 1942-44,
wool, silk, metal, and plastic, ¾ x 23 x 28 in.
overall. Gift of the Mayor's Committee, 1946.89b